HOLY CRAP!

Where's My SUPER Gone?!

Self-Managed Super Made Simple.

AUDREY DAWSON

Holy Crap! Where's My SUPER Gone?!
Self-Managed Simple Made Easy
Author: Audrey Dawson
First published in Australia in 2014
Second edition 2015

Copyright © Audrey Dawson 2014

Publisher: Super Confidence
P.O. Box 199
Annerley Qld 4103
Phone: (617) 3848 0219
Email: info@superconfidence.com.au
Web: www.superconfidence.com.au

The People who make me look good

Edited by: Sara Litchfield – Right Ink on the Wall
www.rightinkonthewall.com

Cover Design: Ryan McDonald-Smith – Younique Creation Web
& Print Design
www.youniquecreation.com

Typeset by: Steven Plummer of SPDesign
spdesign@hargray.com

Printed by: In House Print and Design
www.inhouseprint.com.au

Back Cover Photo: Kerrin Smith
www.kerrinsmith.com.au

DEDICATION

To my late Dad, Clarry Dawson – a true Lancashire gentle man – I dedicate this book to you. Dad, you taught me so much and were there for me when I needed picking up all throughout my life. Thank you. I know you would be immensely proud that your daughter has written a book and yep I'm pretty chuffed myself.

ACKNOWLEDGEMENTS

"There is nothing to writing. All you do is
sit down at a typewriter and bleed."
— ERNEST HEMINGWAY

I COULDN'T AGREE MORE. There was a lot of blood, sweat, gnashing of teeth, pulling of hair and tears that was part of writing this book and that was before I even put one word to paper. Behind a writer though stands a group of people who have shaped that writer and helped them in some way to produce the book. For me, without them, I doubt that I would ever have had the confidence, discipline, sheer determination or madness to have written a book. Thank you, Thank You, Thank You.

❤ To my lovely Mum Margaret – well you were instrumental really – you created the first ingredient – the writer herself and then you taught me discipline and the good old Scottish tenacity and work ethic.

❤ To MGGGGGH Laurie who supports me in every way, even though he says he needs an assistant, and has also lovingly proof read my book; I owe you so much.

❤ To my two gorgeous sons - Sam and Jake – you keep me well and truly grounded and are part of my DNA. (I know you'll be suitably embarrassed so my job is done ☺)

❤ To my sister Pat, King Gaz, Conly and Alix – just for being family and all that entails.

❤ To Rach – my surrogate daughter – for that big laugh and bigger personality and being such an important part of the family.

❤ To Sara, Ryan, Kerrin and Steven – for your incredible creativity.

❤ To Gary for being a great friend, sounding board and for proof reading.

❤ To Heather and Geoff - for being great friends and the photograph that I wrote to.

❤ To the sisterhood – the BGITW – for your support and your friendship.

❤ To Gerry, Avril and Alison – for being inspirational people.

♥ The KPI team, my accountability group and especially the unbelievable Andrew Griffiths who is the greatest mentor I could ever have had and without you, this book would never even have got started. You are a great man Sir.

And finally to you the reader, I humbly thank you for even picking up the book and getting this far. Thank you hopefully for wanting to be empowered and have control and maybe my book will go some way to you having the confidence to say "Yes I can."

TABLE OF CONTENTS

INTRODUCTION

WHEN I FIRST started auditing self-managed super funds (SMSFs), I'd been an auditor for 20 odd years. This being the case, I thought, "How hard can this be?" I've got lots of experience, but it didn't take me too long to see how intricate the wonderful world of self-managed super funds can be. *Complicated* and *complex* are the two words that I would use to describe them, which is also what makes them so interesting.

I thought to myself, "If *I* find it complicated, with all my experience, how does someone with a self-managed super fund or someone thinking of investing in one feel?" What I observed pretty quickly was that, because people with self-managed super funds didn't entirely understand them and didn't know what they didn't know, they were willing to entrust all of their life savings to their advisors – their financial planners and accountants. And that can be a very risky thing to do. There have been many documented cases where this has resulted in people losing everything they have worked so hard for.

Being a frustrated teacher, I thought, "Why not try to get those with self-managed super funds, or those looking at entering this world, to *want* to take more responsibility and have more control over their investment?" That way, when you reach that magical retirement time, you can look back and feel a sense of achievement. You have ensured that you can enjoy your retirement to the fullest.

So I decided to write a book that is not a text book (how off-putting would that be? Even picking up a book like that I can see your eyes glaze over). What I wanted to write was a simple and easy-to-understand guide of the basics – everything that you need to know to be able to start that journey to having a more proactive role in managing your own self-managed super fund. I want you to have a strong foundation, to want to know more and build on your knowledge so that *you* are in control – not your financial planner and your accountant.

I've been auditing self-managed super funds for only a short time compared with other professionals in the industry, so part of me doubted that I could write a book on the subject. When I thought about it, though, I realised my great advantage: although I have built up a strong knowledge of self-managed super funds, I haven't become so totally absorbed technically that I've lost the ability to empathise with you as the owner or prospective owner of one. I can feel your pain.

This book is about the good (the great tax rate and you in control), the bad (the technical jargon and the ever-changing government rules) and the ugly (what happens if it all goes pear shaped?).

Hopefully, I have sparked your interest and that's why you bought this book. Even better, you may have been *given* this book. Either way, just like your home or your SMSF, it could be one of the best investments you've ever made.

So, let's begin the journey…

CHAPTER 1

THAT'S WHY THEY CALL IT A SELF-MANAGED SUPER FUND

WHAT WAS THE reason that you went into a self-managed super fund? Was it because your accountant or financial planner told you to? If I had a dollar for every time that this was the case then I would be an extremely rich person. Or, maybe because you lost a lot of your precious superannuation balance during the global financial crisis, you thought, "Surely I can do better than that?" I know myself my balance reduced by about $30,000 and it takes a long time to claw your money back.

Or you're in a mainstream retail or industry super fund, or what is termed an **APRA regulated superannuation fund**, and probably disappointed with the returns you are seeing with your fund. You want to have greater control over your investment, which seems to be a growing trend, with almost 30,000 self-managed super funds being created each year in Australia.

So, you talk to your accountant and financial planner and organise the set up of a self-managed super fund and for them to manage it. You obviously want to be more in control, which is such a great thing – love it. It's the old *master of your own destiny* stuff.

Why is it, then, that you let your accountant and/or financial planner manage your fund? Here you are with a chance to control your future and you choose not to.

Apart from your home, superannuation is probably the biggest investment that you will make in your life. When it comes to your home, would you allow someone to come in and completely dictate what happens to it? Sure, you have architects and interior designers, but would you go and say to them, "Okay, I want to build a house or do a renovation and here's the money. You guys just go and do it and let me know when it's all finished." I think you know the answer to that. So why would you do it with such an important aspect of your life – your retirement?

When I suggest taking control yourself, does your mind come up with a list of "Buts?"

- But it's easier to leave it to the people who know;

- But it's so complicated with all that technical jargon, plus the government keeps changing the rules;

- But I don't think I have the time to manage it.

You don't want to take control of your super fund because it is hard and it is complicated. Your trusted advisors probably didn't tell you that, did they? If you knew what you know now, do you think that you would have made the same decision to invest in a self-managed super fund? That's a whole different conversation for another time. Right now, if you have a self-managed super fund, you really need to take control. Why? Well, how can I put this subtly? **IT'S CALLED A SELF-MANAGED SUPER FUND FOR A REASON!**

Chapter 2 will give you the basics that you absolutely need to know, and you can also find a glossary guide of terms and information at the back of the book in Appendix A to help you out. But for now, let me again just answer this question: "Why do *you* need to take control?" another way. Tough love lesson number one – *you* are ultimately responsible for your super fund. Not your accountant. Not your financial advisor.

Let me explain – your super fund is what is called a **trust account**. It is a trust account because the money in there is to be kept or held in trust for you until you retire. So it's your money, but it's not *really* yours until you retire. For example, before you retire, you can't take money out to pay off a debt that you might have personally. If you were in a mainstream retail super fund, you would not be able to ring them up and say that you have a car loan that you would like to pay off or a holiday that you would like to take and want the money out of your super fund to do that. The mainstream retail super fund holds your super-annuation in trust for you until you retire and can't release it until then. So of course they would say no. The rules of a self-managed super fund are no different.

The trust account is looked after by people who are called **trustees**. In the case of your self-managed super fund, that is you and whoever else is a member of your super fund.

Now there are, of course, rules (too many of them, you will say) that dictate what you can and can't do with your self-managed super fund. The Australian Tax Office (ATO) makes sure you are abiding by the rules and, if you're not, there can be a whole lot of pain. This can be in the form of fees and fines or, even worse, jail, which I'll touch upon in more detail later. The point I want to make here is this: if something does go wrong, do you think that the ATO will come after your accountant or your financial advisor? Surprise, surprise – no, they won't. They will come after you as trustee of the super fund.

Yes, you can probably seek legal revenge against your accountant or your financial advisor by suing them. But imagine the time, money and pain involved. And how do you think that will leave your poor old self-managed super fund balance? There goes your "happily ever after."

I want you to understand the importance of taking control so you don't have to utter those fateful words: "Holy Crap! Where's my super gone?"

With control also comes responsibility. Do your advisors understand all the rules and regulations and your role and responsibilities? Have they explained them to you? This probably gives you an indication as to what their knowledge-level is.

By demystifying some of the complications of super funds, this book should make you feel more comfortable about wanting to take control, knowing what your role and responsibilities are, and knowing what important rules and regulations you need to be aware of. You've already learnt your first lesson about self-managed super funds – that *you* are trustee of your fund and *you* are responsible for it.

This chapter sets the mantra for the book and I will keep repeating it throughout until you get sick of hearing it. It'll be worth it, as long as you get it.

MANTRA
THERE'S A REASON THEY CALL IT A SELF-MANAGED SUPER FUND

You are the trustee of your super fund and *you* are ultimately responsible for your super fund. Not your accountant. Not your financial planner. Isn't that the best reason to take control? Just remember, with control comes responsibility.

CHAPTER 2

NEED-TO-KNOW – WHAT ARE THE BASICS?

CHAPTER 1 WAS all about the importance of taking control and proactively managing your self-managed super fund. In this chapter, I will be starting to explain the basics of how you do that.

Demystifying those complicated terms

I'm not advocating that you go solo in managing your fund – you still need your financial planners and accountants as trusted advisors. But *advisors* is the operative word. *Manager* should be your title.

You need to be able to ask the right questions of your advisors. How can you do that when you don't know what you don't know? I was in your shoes when I first started auditing self-managed super funds. The key was slowly building up my knowledge. This meant lots and lots of research. I have a lever arch file where I keep all my important information, which I can and do refer to regularly. It's broken up into a number of sections that represent the main pieces of knowledge I need when I'm auditing a super fund. I would like to share the basic pieces of knowledge with you on the start of your journey to proactively managing your own super fund. If you have a file of easy-to-understand information that makes sense, you will have more of a chance of remembering it.

With the right basic knowledge you can start to ask the right questions. This chapter will begin to present you with the Basic Pieces of Knowledge (BPKs) you need. I have included the BPKs that appear in the following chapters in a glossary of important information, located at the back of the book at Appendix A. Hopefully, this will provide a handy reference guide to flick back to, just like my file.

We'll begin by exploring some basic terminology that you need to understand. I will include a rundown of the rules and I will highlight the important terms.

Please be mindful that the rules are relevant to the 2015 - 16 financial year. As you know, one of the frustrating things about superannuation is the fact that the government keeps changing the rules. They often indicate they will change not only the rules but also the amounts allowable under the rules. And then they change their minds. So nothing is set in concrete. I will include figures that may change, however, they *will* remain in the ball park. What I want you to get out of these pieces of knowledge are the basics of what a super fund is about and the basic rules. When you are up to speed with the basics, you'll be in a great position to build on that knowledge and stay on top of any changes to the rules that affect your super fund.

So you don't feel swamped, I've categorised these BPKs into four bite-sized areas and these will be covered in the next few chapters:

- What are the basic foundations of a SMSF?
            - this Chapter

- What can you put into your SMSF?
            - Chapter 3

- What's involved in the everyday operation of your SMSF?   - Chapter 4

- How do you access your SMSF?
            - Chapter 5

Foundations Of A Self-Managed Super Fund

The first important step in building your basic knowledge is to learn the overarching structure of a self-managed super fund. This will make up your first 5 BPKs.

BPK#1 – Trust Account

You already learned your first bit of terminology in Chapter 1. Your super fund is a **trust account** and you are the **trustee** of that trust account. Your super fund is a trust account because the money in there is to be kept or held *in trust* for you until you retire.

BPK#2 – Individual Trustee Or Corporate Trustee

In a self-managed super fund it is possible to either have individual trustees or a corporate trustee.

In an **individual trustee** structure, all other members of your super fund will also be trustees.

Alternatively, it's possible your accountant or financial planner has arranged for a company to be set up and it's that company that is the trustee of the super fund. The company is known as a **corporate trustee**. Where a company is set up as a trustee, you will be a director of the company, as will any other members of the super fund.

In Chapter 1, I also stressed that you, as trustee, are responsible for your trust account / self-managed super fund. The ATO wants to ensure that you acknowledge this and so, to be a trustee of your super fund, you have to sign a **trustee declaration form.** The declaration aims to ensure that you, as trustee or as director of a corporate trustee, understand your obligations and responsibilities.

As trustee, your role is to ensure that the super fund is adhering to the legislative rules and regulations. One of the fundamental rules you need to enforce is that the fund is being maintained and managed for the sole purpose of providing for the members' retirement. This is known as the **sole purpose test**.

There are pros and cons of having individual trustees as opposed to a corporate trustee. It is less costly being an individual trustee, as to set up a corporate trustee you have to set up a company, and there will be ongoing fees associated with maintaining the company.

The cons of being an individual trustee, however, definitely outweigh the pros. The main disadvantage is that trustees are responsible for what happens in the super fund. If anything goes wrong, they are personally liable. There are a couple of true-life examples that illustrate this point really well.

The first is the *Triway Superannuation Fund*, in which a mother, father and son were members and trustees of the super fund. The son, who was a drug addict, took almost all the money out of the super fund before being entitled to it. He also declared himself bankrupt while remaining one of the trustees of the super fund, which is also not allowed. The ATO, who have a regulatory role in relation to self-managed super funds, made the fund non-compliant and fined the trustees. Because they were individual trustees and there was effectively no money left in the super fund, the trustees were personally responsible for the payment of the fines. The trustees appealed the decision to the Administrative Appeals Tribunal (AAT) but were unsuccessful. The AAT ruled that they, as trustees, were personally responsible for the tax and fines.

The other example is the *Shail Superannuation Fund*, in which the trustees and members were Mr and Mrs Shail.

They were divorced but had remained trustees of their two member super fund. Mr Shail withdrew $3,460,000 (almost all the balance) from the super fund without being entitled to it, and moved to Turkey, without telling Mrs Shail. The ATO made the fund non-compliant and, as a result, the super fund had a tax bill of $1,583,873.69, plus penalties of $1,475,322.50.

Mrs Shail, in her capacity as trustee of the super fund, appealed the decision to the AAT on the grounds that she was not aware of the breach, did not consent to it and did not benefit from it. The AAT upheld the decision made by the ATO. Their decision centred around the fact that each trustee is equally responsible for the decision making in the super fund. Given that there was practically no money left in the super fund, Mrs Shail was personally responsible for paying the $3.06 million in tax and fines. Mr Shail appears to have escaped liability by being overseas.

Isn't that scary? In both cases, had there been a corporate trustee, it would have been the company that was liable for the tax and fines, not the individuals.

From 1 July 2014 the penalties for certain legislative breaches were beefed up. An example is a breach of the lending rules i.e. the trustees lend or provide financial assistance to a member or relative. The penalty imposed is $10,200. It there are individual trustees, each of the individual trustees will have to personally pay the $10,200 fine. If on the other hand there is a corporate trustee, then the corporate trustee is liable for only one fine of $10,200. It is important to note that your super fund cannot pay these penalties.

Another advantage of having a corporate trustee is administrative in nature. If there are any changes to membership, it will not be necessary to change documents like the trust deed, or ownership details in relation to assets of the super fund.

If you chose to have a corporate trustee for your super fund, I would recommend that you don't use a company that you have already set up for a business for example. That is because, if something does go wrong, then like the individual trustee situation, the company would be responsible and any assets of the company could be taken into consideration. It is better to have a corporate trustee that is set up solely as trustee of your super fund.

BPK#3 – Membership

You play two roles in your super fund – you are a trustee, either as an individual or as a director of a company set up as trustee, and you are also a **member** of the super fund. These are two very distinct roles, so you wear two very distinct hats. Your trustee hat is described in BPK#2.

As a member, your role is to contribute to the fund and reap the benefits when you retire. Most self-managed super funds have two members, usually husband and wife or *de facto* partners. For those that aren't the norm, just be aware that there are rules as to how many members can be in a super fund. At present, the maximum number of members is four.

All members must be either an individual trustee or a director of the corporate trustee. All trustees do not, however, have to be members, e.g. for a single member fund, where it is an individual trustee structure, there must be two trustees and one of these will be a non-member.

In BPK#2, I covered some of the advantages of having a corporate trustee and I just want to mention here another advantage. If any member leaves the fund and there is only one member left, you don't have to replace them, as the corporate trustee can have a single director with a single member fund. In an individual trustee structure, there must always be two individual trustees.

An annual **member's statement** is prepared for each member. The information that should be contained in your member's statement includes:

- Opening balance.

- Increase in member's account during the finan-cial year from such things as contributions (explained in Chapter 3, BPK#6), transfers in (explained in Chapter 3, BPK#12) and share of net earnings (covered in Chapter 4, BPK#16).

- Decrease in member's account during the year from such things as benefits paid (covered in Chapter 5, various BPK's), tax (covered in Chapter 4, BPK#14) and insurance policy pre-miums paid (covered in Chapter 4, BPK#16).

- Closing balance.

- Classification of closing balance into preserved, restricted non-preserved and unrestricted non-preserved (explained in Chapter 4, BPK#13).

- Tax free and taxable components (explained in Chapter 4, BPK#13).

BPK #4 – Legislation And Being A Complying Fund

As with any kind of industry, there are overarching rules that dictate how self-managed super funds are to operate. This is in the form of an act and regulations. At the moment that act is called the **Superannuation Industry (Supervision) Act 1993** and the relevant regulations are called **Superannuation Industry (Supervision) Regulations 1994**. I'm not suggesting that you read them (I suspect if you did you would be stabbing your eye out with a pencil before too long). I just want you to be aware of them (and I have summarised the sections that I concentrate on when I audit a self-managed super fund in the back, at Appendix B).

To be classified as a **complying fund** simply means that it's been acknowledged that your super fund follows all the rules that are detailed in the legislation. I'll cover what the important rules are throughout this book so you can have the confidence that your accountant and/or financial planner are doing the right thing. This is important, because if your super fund is not following the rules and the ATO finds out, then you can be classified as a **non-complying fund**. That means the super fund can be taxed at very high rates, which at present is 45%. Imagine what that would do to your super fund balance and, ultimately, your goal of being able to enjoy your retirement to the fullest. Can you see why it is so important to proactively manage your self-managed super fund?

BPK #5 – Trust Deed

As well as the overarching legislative requirements, each and every super fund needs to have its own set of rules. This comes in the form of a **trust deed**. This is an important document and it should mirror the contents of the relevant act and regulations. There are numerous companies that will prepare these for you. They can be generic, off-the-shelf documents or be tailor made to the circumstances of your super fund. If you already have a self-managed super fund, I suspect that you probably have an off-the-shelf trust deed that was arranged by your accountant/financial planner and you signed it where they put the "sign here" sticker. Again, they are quite a complex document and you probably won't be inclined to want to read them, but what I will emphasise is that, whatever is happening in your super fund, you need to be sure that your trust deed allows it. An example would be where you decide that you want to buy a piece of art. Your trust deed needs to have clauses to allow your fund to do this.

Another example is paying a pension. I know that sounds silly. You would think that your trust deed would include that automatically. Isn't that what a super fund is all about? Let me tell you, as an auditor of self-managed super funds, the trust deed is one of the documents that I always read, and I have found a number of times that the type of pension the super fund is paying has not been covered in the trust deed. Where it has not been covered, it is not allowed, and the fund should not be doing it. The consequences are that I'm obliged to report it to the ATO as part of my audit. So it's probably a good idea that you get familiar with your super fund's trust deed.

MANTRA
THERE'S A REASON THEY CALL IT A SELF-MANAGED SUPER FUND

You are the trustee of your super fund and *you* are ultimately responsible for your super fund. Not your accountant. Not your financial planner. Isn't that the best reason to take control? Just remember, with control comes responsibility.

Things you need to remember about the basic foundations of your self-managed super fund

1. You deserve to enjoy your retirement to the fullest.

2. It's about being able to ask the right questions, which is hard when you don't know what you don't know.

3. If you have the basic knowledge, you can start to ask the right questions.

4. Your self-managed super fund is a trust account, with the money being held in trust for you as a member of the super fund until you are entitled to receive it.

5. Your super fund's trust deed is the document that dictates what your super fund can and can't do. Whatever is happening in your super fund, please be sure that your super fund trust deed allows it.

6. You play two very distinct roles, with very different responsibilities, in your super fund – you are a trustee and you are also a member of your super fund.

7. As trustee, either as an individual or as a director of a company set up as trustee, your role is to ensure that the super fund is adhering to the legislative rules and regulations. You need to ensure that the fund is being maintained and managed for the sole purpose of providing for the members' retirement. This is known as the sole purpose test.

8. As a member, your role is to contribute to the fund and reap the benefits when you retire.

9. Currently, the maximum number of members allowed in a self-managed super fund is four.

10. Every member must be either an individual trustee or a director of the corporate trustee. All trustees do not, however, have to be members, e.g. in a single member fund with an individual trustee structure, there must be two trustees and one of these will be a non-member.

CHAPTER 3

CONTRIBUTIONS – WHAT CAN YOU PUT INTO YOUR SELF-MANAGED SUPER FUND?

WHAT IS PUT into a self-managed super fund is called a contribution. Contributions come in different forms, are classified differently and are, of course, taxed differently. There are limits on the amount that can be contributed into a super fund. That's what you will learn about in this chapter.

BPK#6 – Different Types Of Contributions

At the present time, the following types of contributions are allowable:

1. Generally, if you work for someone, are over 18 and you earn more than $450 a month (before

tax), your employer has to pay a certain percentage of your salary in the form of superannuation. These are known as **mandatory contributions or super guarantee contributions**. For the 2015-16 financial year this is 9.5% of your salary. This will stay the same until 30 June 2021 and then it will increase by .5% until it reaches 12%.

2. You, as an employee, can also choose to have part of your salary paid into superannuation and this is referred to as **salary sacrificing.**

3. If you are self-employed, you are not required to contribute to a super fund. However, if you do, these are classed as **self-employed contributions.**

4. You can contribute additional amounts into superannuation and these are called **personal contributions.**

5. If you are classified as a low income earner and you make personal contributions into superannuation, then the government will match or co-contribute up to $500 of the contribution you have made. These are referred to as **government co-contributions.**

6. Your spouse can contribute into your super fund. These are given the obvious name of **spouse contributions.** There are tax advantages

in doing this, as your spouse can claim a tax rebate for the contributions made (explained in more detail in BPK#11).

7. Contributions other than cash can be made. These are called **in-specie contributions.** As you would expect, there are a few rules governing in-specie contributions, which I cover in BPK#9.

8. Rollovers or transfers in are amounts moved from other super funds, which I cover in BPK#12.

BPK#7 – Classification Of Contributions And Why It's Important

For mandatory or super guarantee contributions, salary sacrifice and self-employed contributions (points 1-3 above), a tax deduction for those payments will have been claimed by either your employer in their tax return (mandatory or super guarantee contributions) or you in your tax return (self-employed contributions). These are called **concessional contributions**.

In relation to personal contributions (point 4 above) you may or may not have claimed a tax deduction. If a tax deduction has or will be claimed, then this contribution will also be classified as a **concessional contribution.**

For the rest, a tax deduction won't have been claimed and these are known as **non-concessional contributions**.

Why is whether a tax deduction has been claimed important? It's important because that will dictate how the contribution will be taxed in your super fund. If a tax deduction has been claimed before it is paid into your super fund, in the case of concessional contributions, then tax has to be paid by your superfund on those contributions, which at present is 15%. If a tax deduction has not been claimed, in the case of non-concessional contributions, then tax will not be paid by your super fund on those contributions.

I won't go into great detail here, as I cover tax in Chapter 4 (BPK#15). I just want you to be aware that there are rules governing whether contributions are taxed or not. Visually it looks something like this:

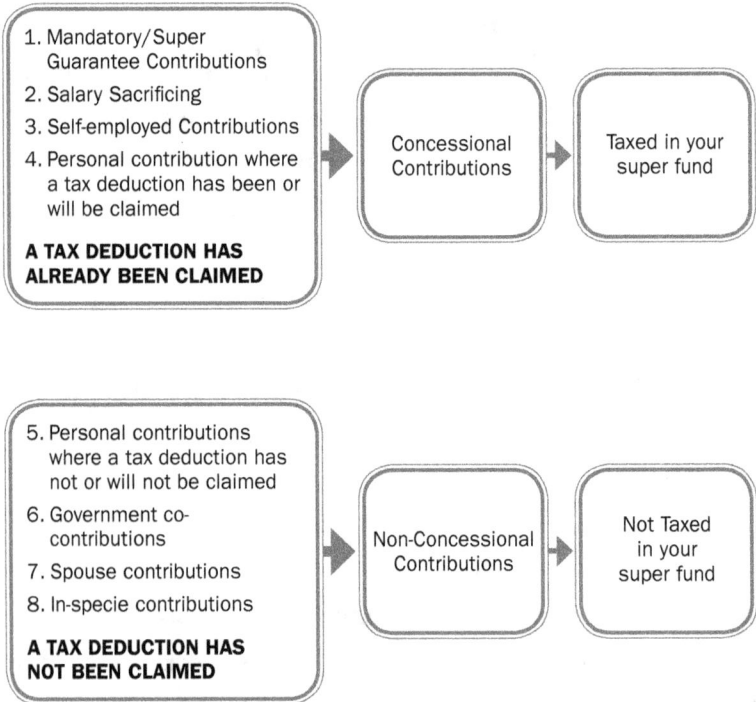

BPK#8 – How Much Can Be Contributed Into Super?

There are limits on the amount of each type of contribution that can be made. This will be affected by how old you are and whether you are classified as still working, so there is not one rule for everyone.

The limits are known as **contribution caps**. To give you an idea regarding the maximum amounts the caps allow, the following are the rules for the 2015-16 financial year:

- **Concessional contributions** – if you are under 50, the maximum for concessional contributions is $30,000 per year. For those aged 50 and over, it is $35,000.

- **Non-concessional contributions** – if you are under 65, the maximum for these contributions is $180,000 a year, or $540,000 over a three year period. The general rule, at the moment, is that non-concessional contributions can be up to six times the amount of concessional contributions that can be contributed. You can pay the entire $540,000 in one year, but will not be able to contribute any more over the following two years. If you are over 65 and less than 75, you have to satisfy the work test. You must be employed for a minimum of 40 hours over 30 consecutive days during the financial year. The maximum is also $180,000 a year, but you can't pay the three years' worth ($540,000) in one year.

- If you are over 75, only the mandatory or super guarantee contributions can be accepted by the super fund.

The contribution caps relating to each of the age groups seem to change each year, so the above is not set in stone. It only relates to the 2015-16 financial year. I've included it as a general indication of what can be contributed into a super fund and to demonstrate that there are ceilings on what can be contributed. If you Google "contribution caps," one of the links you will generate will lead to the ATO website. They will have a table of each of the different contribution caps, relevant age brackets and maximum amounts. If you do that at the start of each financial year, you will be up to date with the current amounts and applicable age brackets.

You need to be careful that you don't exceed whatever the contribution caps are as:

- For concessional contributions the excess amount will automatically be included in your assessable income and be taxed at your marginal rate of tax less the 15% tax that will be paid by your super fund on these contributions; and

- For non-concessional contributions, they are taxed at the top marginal rate of tax which is 49%. The government has recently legislated that, for excess contributions after 1 July 2013, excess amounts plus 85% of the related earnings can paid back to you:15% of the related earnings remain in the super fund to pay the tax on these earnings. You will be taxed at your marginal rate of tax less the 15% tax paid by your super fund.

An important point to remember, as trustee, is to make sure that you, as a member of the fund (remember those different roles and responsibilities), provide the fund with your **tax file number (TFN)**. If the super fund does not have a member's TFN, the relevant rule dictates that you, as trustee, are not able to accept contributions. These would have to be immediately returned if you don't receive the TFN within 30 days. If you don't return the funds, your super fund will be taxed at a much higher rate on those contributions.

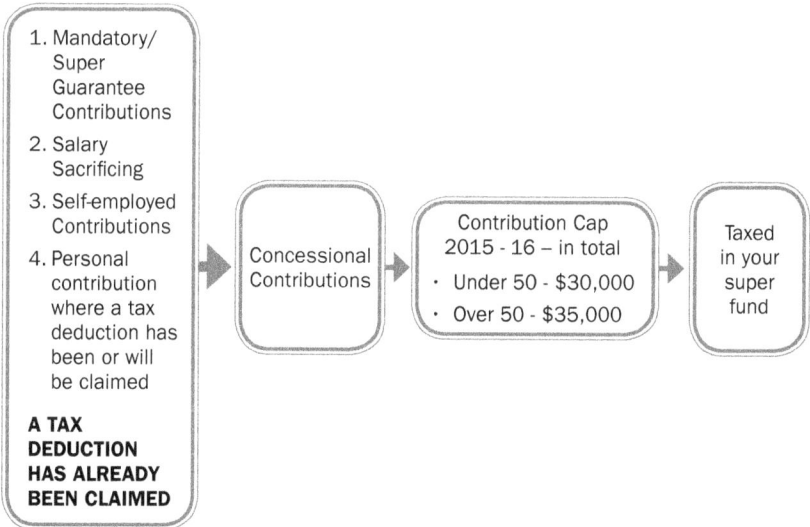

1. Mandatory/ Super Guarantee Contributions
2. Salary Sacrificing
3. Self-employed Contributions
4. Personal contribution where a tax deduction has been or will be claimed

A TAX DEDUCTION HAS ALREADY BEEN CLAIMED

→ Concessional Contributions

→ Contribution Cap 2015 - 16 – in total
· Under 50 - $30,000
· Over 50 - $35,000

→ Taxed in your super fund

```
┌────────────────────┐     ┌──────────────────┐
│ 1. Personal        │     │ Contribution Cap │
│    contributions   │     │ 2015 - 16 (6 times│
│    where a tax     │     │ the concessional │
│    deduction has   │     │ contribution cap)│
│    not or will not │     │ – in total       │
│    be claimed      │     │                  │
│                    │     │ • Under 65 - $180,00│
│ 2. Government      │     │   a year or $540,000│
│    co-             │     │   over a 3 year period│
│    contributions   │     │   – e.g. can pay │
│                    │     │   $540,000 in one│
│ 3. Spouse          │     │   year           │
│    contributions   │     │                  │
│                    │     │ • Between 65 and 75 -│
│ 4. In-specie       │     │   $180,000 a year│
│    contributions   │     │                  │
│                    │     │ • Over 75 – can't│
│ A TAX              │     │   make non       │
│ DEDUCTION          │     │   concessional   │
│ HAS NOT BEEN       │     │   contributions  │
│ CLAIMED            │     │                  │
└────────────────────┘     └──────────────────┘
```

Non-Concessional Contributions → Not Taxed in your super fund

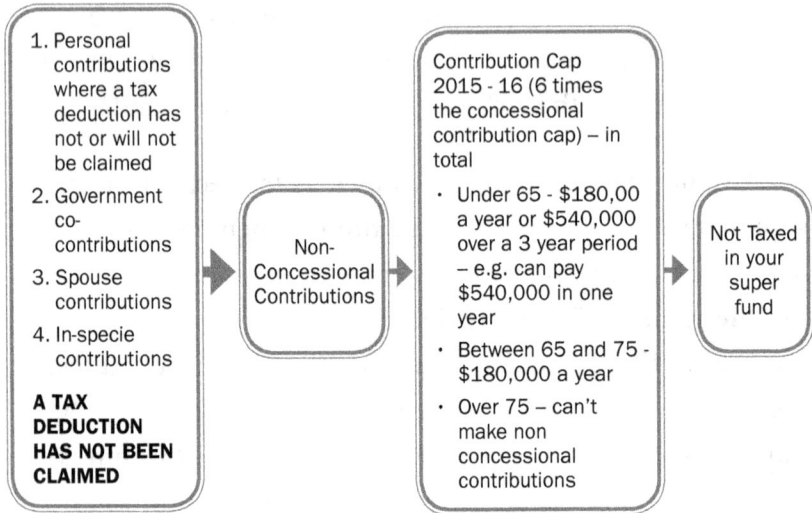

BPK#9 – In-specie Contributions

It's not only cash that can be paid in as a contribution; it is possible for another type of asset to be paid into the fund. An example is shares, which could be transferred in rather than you selling them and then contributing the money. This is an exception to the general rule that your super fund can't acquire any assets from any member or related party of the fund. Don't we love that about self-managed super funds? There's a rule but, wait, it doesn't apply to everything. The exceptions are the following, which can be transferred in as in-specie contributions:

- Shares that are listed on an approved exchange, such as the Australian Stock Exchange;

- Commercial property, which is also known as business real property;

- Units in widely held unit trusts;

- Assets from a member or related party of the trust (**in-house assets**), where the value isn't more than 5% of your super fund's asset value.

When these assets are transferred in, it needs to be at **market value**, which may require an independent valuation. This would definitely be the case for commercial property or in-house assets.

Also remember that the contribution cap rules still apply to in-specie contributions.

Be aware that the person transferring in may be liable for capital gains tax, as the transfer in is treated as though the asset were sold and then purchased by the super fund. Please see your accountant about the taxation implications for all parties.

BPK#10 – Contributions Reserves

It is possible for you, as a member to make contributions to you super fund, in excess of the contribution cap and not be penalised. It works this way; under the legislation, contributions made by or on behalf of a member to a super fund must be allocated to the member's accumulation account within 28 days. It is possible therefore for contributions to be initially posted to an unallocated contribution account or contributions reserve account before being allocated to a member's account within 28 days. Why is this important? Given this time frame, it is possible to make concessional contributions in excess of the contribution cap at the end of a financial year and not be penalised. The advantage of this strategy is that the contributor can claim the tax deduction on the entire amount however there will be no tax paid by the super fund until the contribution is allocated to the member's account. The best way to illustrate this is through an example:

- Contribution Cap for concessional contributions = $35,000

- Member A's total concessional contributions made during 2014-15 and allocated to member's account up to 15 June 2015 = $35,000 which is made up of $10,000 super guarantee employer contributions, $15,000 salary sacrifice and $10,000 personal contribution where a tax deduction has been claimed

- Member A makes an additional personal deductible contribution of $35,000 on 17 June 2015

- This additional $35,000 contribution is posted to an unallocated contribution account/contribution reserve

- For the purposes of the 2014-15 financial year:

  · Member A will be able to claim the $10,000 personal deductible contribution (up to

15 June 2015) plus the $35,000 personal deductible contribution (contribution on 17 June 2015)

· The Super Fund will pay tax on $35,000 concessional contribution paid and allocated to the member's accumulation account

· No tax is payable on $35,000 which has been posted to the unallocated contribution account.

• For the purposes of the 2015-16 financial year:

· The Super Fund will allocate the $35,000 to the member's account as a concessional contribution by 28 July 2015

· Tax will be paid by the Super Fund on this contribution

As a word of caution, the ATO has realised this is happening and has documented their view on the subject. It's not an easy document to read in its entirety, believe me. So to simplify it: the ATO recognises that these arrangements are occurring and have ruled that your super fund would be required to still include the contributions in the tax return of the financial year in which they are actually paid into your super fund. This will of course trigger the excess contributions cap scenario and the related tax consequences. Your super fund will then have to raise an objection with the ATO on the grounds that it has been assessed incorrectly in relation to the excessive contributions cap. As you can see, there are definitely some hoops that you need to jump through in relation to utilising a contributions reserve and you need to consider these before making the decision that you want your super fund to go down this path, should your financial advisor recommend it.

As always – please make sure that your trust deed allows your super fund to have a reserve.

BPK#11 – Contribution Splitting

Where your spouse is also a member of your self-managed super fund, it is possible for you to split your **concessional contributions** with them (employer, salary sacrificing, personal contributions where a tax deduction has or will be claimed and self-employed contributions). An advantage of this would be if your spouse is older and will be eligible to access their superannuation benefits sooner; this means it is better that the concessional contributions are given or attributed to them and can be accessed sooner. Alternatively, if you are nearing retirement, it may assist with possible Centrelink payments if contributions are split to a younger member.

Contributions splitting operates as follows: your concessional contributions are paid in and show as being your contributions in the super fund in the financial year that they are paid in. Anywhere in the next financial year, you can nominate to assign some or all of your **concessional contributions** from the prior year to your spouse, up to the post-tax amount, which is the amount contributed less the tax that your super fund has paid (15%).

Let me give you an example:

Gary (58) and his wife Patricia (55) have a self-managed super fund and are both working. Gary's concessional contributions, through payments from his employer and salary sacrificing, in the 2014-15 financial year, amount to $10,000; whilst Patricia's concessional contributions are $9,000. Gary is planning on retiring at 60, so it is more advantageous that all concessional contributions be attributed to Gary, as he will be accessing his superannuation benefits sooner than Patricia. In the 2015-16 financial year, Patricia can split or attribute part or all of her concessional contributions to Gary, up to the post-tax amount. This would amount to 85% of the concessional contribution, as 15% tax is paid by the super fund on concessional contributions (Refer BPK#15 Taxation). In this case, the maximum that Patricia could split or assign to Gary would be 85% of $9,000, or $7,650. When Gary receives the $7,650 in the 2015-16 financial year, it is classified as a contribution splitting contribution and does not affect Gary's concessional or non-concessional caps.

Other rules that you need to know are:

- It only happens once a year, always in the financial year following the one in which the concessional contributions were paid in;

- You can't split your contributions if your spouse has already retired; and

- A Contribution Splitting Notice form has to be completed. You, as trustee, need to ensure that this occurs. This form is available from the Australian Taxation Office website.

BPK#12 – Rollovers And Transfers In

When you set up your self-managed super fund, you may have transferred in the superannuation balance from your previous superannuation fund. There are no barriers, such as age or employment status, to being able to rollover into a self-managed super fund. And the same rules apply regarding access these funds, i.e. you will not be able to access the balance until you are entitled to it, when you attain a **condition of release**. You will learn more about that in Chapter 5, which is about how you can access your super fund.

There is, of course, an inevitable form that you will have to fill out in order to rollover. Again, this is available from the Australian Tax Office website.

Hopefully, you are slowly building your knowledge in relation to how self-managed super funds work. In the next chapter, you will find out what happens while you are contributing and before you can access your super fund.

MANTRA
THERE'S A REASON THEY CALL IT A
SELF-MANAGED SUPER FUND

You **are the trustee of your super fund and** *you* **are ultimately responsible for your super fund. Not your accountant. Not your financial planner. Isn't that the best reason to take control? Just remember, with control comes responsibility.**

Things you need to remember about contributions

1. Concessional contributions are employer mandatory contributions, super guarantee contributions, salary sacrificing, personal contributions where a tax deduction has or will be claimed and self-employed contributions.

2. Non-concessional contributions are personal contributions where a tax deduction has not been claimed, government co-contributions, spouse contributions and in-specie contributions.

3. Concessional contributions are taxable and non-concessional contributions are tax free in the hands of your super fund.

4. There are limits on the amount of concessional and non-concessional contributions that can be made to a self-managed super fund, which are referred to as contribution caps.

49

5. You can make in-specie (other than cash) contributions into your super fund, but these are generally limited to shares and commercial property.

6. Your super fund has to have your tax file number (TFN) to accept contributions, from you, as a member.

7. Contributions can be split.

8. Your super fund can accept rollovers or transfers in from other superannuation funds.

CHAPTER 4

OPERATION – HOW DOES YOUR SELF-MANAGED SUPER FUND TICK ALONG?

So, you have your self-managed super fund and there are contributions being paid into it. What happens next? That is what I'll cover off in this chapter.

BPK#13 – The Phases And Classification Of Your Super Fund Balance

Accumulation Phase and Pension Phase

While you are still working and not receiving any benefits from your super fund, your super fund is in the **accumulation phase**. All members of your super fund will have their own **accumulation account**, which records

their balance. This is updated each year with their contributions, share of earnings/losses, any expenses directly
attributable to them and applicable tax. Each member will
receive details of their balance annually in the form of a
Members Statement (as described in BPK#3).

The only other phase is the **pension phase**, which begins
when you are eligible to take the money out of your super
fund and you nominate to do so. This will be covered in
Chapter 5.

Tax Free and Taxable Components

Each member's **accumulation account** balance will
comprise a **tax free component** and a **taxable component.**
These components are dependent on whether a tax deduction has been claimed on the contributions made. I covered
these kind of contributions in Chapter 3 and it will probably be handy to go over them again.

The **tax free component** comprises the member's non-
concessional contributions, which includes personal contributions where a tax deduction has not been claimed,
government co-contributions, spouse contributions and in-
specie contributions. Given that the relevant amount of tax
has been paid on these prior to them being contributed to
your super fund, there will be no further tax payable.

The **taxable component** relates to the concessional
contributions, such as employer contributions, salary sacrificing, personal contributions where a tax deduction has
or will be claimed and self-employed contributions, as well
as any share of net earnings, plus tax and expenses directly

attributable to the member. A deduction has been claimed on these contributions and the only tax that has been paid is by the super fund, which is at a low rate.

In the taxable category, it is also possible to have contributions where there has been no tax paid at all, an example being where a member pays in the proceeds of an insurance claim, where a tax deduction has been claimed on the premiums paid. Another example is the rolling over of a defined benefit from a corporate or government fund into the accumulation fund. These would be rare. These contributions are classified as being an **untaxed element.** Self-managed super funds can't have untaxed elements as part of the accumulation balance so these would be taxed at 15% in the year they are received into the superfund.

This is important information when your super fund starts to pay out retirement benefits, which I'll cover in more detail in Chapter 5.

Preserved, Restricted Non-Preserved and Unrestricted Non-Preserved – What the heck are they?

There is also the need to classify the benefits in your super fund for each member in relation to what stage of the super life they are in – accumulation, pension phase or the ability to be in the pension phase. Why? Because this will dictate whether you, as a member, can access them.

This area seemed really confusing to me initially. When I read that your superannuation fund balance can be classified as **preserved, restricted non-preserved** or **unrestricted**

non-preserved, I totally tuned out, my eyes glazed over and I thought "What the…?" Like so much of the language in superannuation, I think the government uses deliberately unusual or long-winded names that are there to force you to tune out. When I dug below the surface, though, I realised that this area wasn't as bad as it seemed. I'll simplify it for you so that you'll see that it isn't too hard to understand.

The funds that are in your super fund will be classified as **preserved** or **non-preserved.**

While your super fund is in the accumulation phase, the funds are generally classified as **preserved.** They are preserved because they are the part of your super fund that you can't touch. You simply cannot access them. This is a rule, which I'll call the **preservation rule,** which was introduced on 1 July 1999.

There is, of course, the inevitable exception and this is in relation to any contributions paid into super prior to 1 July 1999, before the preservation rule came into being. These contributions are classified as **restricted non-preserved.** You're probably wondering, "Can I have them or not?" You **can** access these funds, but it is restricted to when you can legally access them, which is in the event you cease working for an employer who was making those contributions for you prior to 1 July 1999. So, if you were working for an employer prior to 1 July 1999 and resigned after that date, then you can access any benefits paid prior to 1 July 1999 and you don't have to be over your preservation age. (refer BPK#20)

The last category is **unrestricted non-preserved** funds. As the name suggests, there are no restrictions on the super fund paying these funds to you. This happens when you reach 65, or if you have previously met a condition of release but have so far chosen not to take the funds.

These categories will also be included in your annual **member's statement**, which is included in the financial statements that are prepared for your super fund (as described in BPK#3).

BPK#14 – Investments

This is probably one of the biggest reasons you went into a self-managed super fund – the variety of things you can invest in. Some examples are:

- Putting the cash that your super fund is accumulating in the bank or investing in a term deposit.

- Shares – these can range from blue chip to high risk.

- Property – this is becoming more and more popular. I cover it in detail later in Chapter 7 (on borrowing) and Chapter 11 (on bad advice), because there is a lot you need to know about this one.

- Taxi licences.

- Vending machines.

- Investing in your passions – you can purchase **collectibles or personal use assets** such as art, collectible firearms (not the illegal ones), wine or spirits, antiques, postage stamps, motor vehicles, recreational boats, sporting memorabilia and jewellery. The big rule here is that you, or any related party, can't enjoy or use these collectibles whilst you are in your **accumulation phase**. This means that you, or a related party, can't wear the jewellery, hang the art in your home or office, drink the wine, drive the car or sail the boat. That can't happen until you retire. **Related parties** include a spouse, relatives, any partnerships that you might be in, or any trusts and companies that you, or another member of the fund, controls.

The ATO has taken a tough stance on collectibles because it is so hard to police and there's a high risk that members of a super fund will use or enjoy an asset before retirement. It's a whole lot of temptation. There are now new rules that if you purchase them, you have to insure them within a week of purchase, have them valued annually and have to organise suitable storage for them, which can't be at your home or office. You will need written proof of where you stored a collectible, as well as documentation of the reasons for the decision on where you decided to store it. These new rules came in for purchases of collectibles after 2011. If you purchased any prior to that, you will have until 1 July 2016 to abide by the new rules. It seems like the ATO is hoping that these new rules will be enough of a deterrent to stop super funds investing in these types of assets altogether.

A few points that you need to remember are:

- Your trust deed governs what you can and can't do in your super fund and, therefore, must allow you to invest in whatever you're investing in. It's your responsibility to make sure it does;

- Any investment has to be in the name of the super fund; and

- Don't ever forget the **sole purpose test,** which dictates that your fund is maintained for the sole purpose of providing for your retirement, not for satisfying your passion for boats, cars, art or wine. You, as trustee of your super fund, must ensure that any investment decisions are in line with the ultimate prize – providing for your retirement so that you can enjoy it to the fullest.

BPK#15 – Taxation

Yep, death and taxes – the two certainties in life. Your super fund is no different to an individual, business or a company in that it is liable for tax. Tax is payable on the **concessional contributions** that are made into the super fund and on its earnings whilst in accumulation phase. Your super fund is required to submit a tax return to the ATO.

One of the great advantages of putting your money into super is that the tax rate is low, presently 15%.

To clarify some of the other things you need to know about how tax works in a super fund, the following is a summary of the rules that apply, some of which I've touched on previously:

- **Concessional contributions** – We covered concessional contributions in Chapter 3. To recap, these are contributions from your employer, salary sacrificing, personal contributions where a tax deduction has or will be claimed or self-employed contributions. In these cases, a tax deduction has been claimed. Whatever concessional contributions are paid into a super fund, the super fund has to pay 15% tax on these.

- **Non-concessional contributions** – Also covered in Chapter 3, these are contributions like personal contributions where a tax deduction has not been claimed, government co-contributions, spouse contributions and in-specie contributions. A tax deduction has not been claimed on these contributions and this means that your super fund doesn't have to pay tax on these contributions.

- Your super fund is, hopefully, earning money through the fund's investments. The earnings may include interest earned, or rent received, if your super fund has, say, a term deposit or a commercial property. The super fund can claim the expenses that it incurs in the course of earning that interest or rent. The earnings less the expenses give what is termed the **net income or earnings**. Your super will pay 15% tax on these net income or earnings. It can get a bit complicated, and this is definitely where you need the professionals.

Your super fund will be able to take advantage of this low tax environment as long as your fund is classified as a **complying fund** (BPK#3), i.e. it is found to be adhering to the legislative requirements and following the rules. A **non-complying fund** is taxed at a very high, penalty rate, which at present is 45%.

BPK#16 – Allocation Of Earnings And Contributions

Your super fund will earn money from its investments, which, along with contributions, is how your fund grows. Each year, these contributions and net earnings or losses need to be allocated to each member's accumulation account.

The balances that each member has in the super fund are probably not equal, so it is important that the net earnings or losses are allocated in a fair and reasonable way.

This is also a requirement set out in the **Superannuation Industry (Supervision) Regulations 1994.** What is fair and reasonable? In general, the allocation for a financial year will be based on the percentage of the total balance that each member has at the beginning of the financial year.

As an example, let's say Heather and Geoff have a self-managed super fund and the total balance of the super fund at the start of the 2014-15 financial year is $450,000. Heather has an individual balance of $100,000 and Geoff has an individual balance of $350,000. The percentages that would be applicable for the allocation of the net earnings or the losses for the 2014-15 financial year would be 22% to Heather (100,000/450,000) and 78% to Geoff (350,000/450,000).

This allocation percentage will only be applicable to the **net income or earnings** (revenue less the general expenses) and to the tax that relates to the net earnings, because these are attributable to all the members.

Any concessional or non-concessional contributions that each member makes, or has made on their behalf, and any expenses that relate directly to the member, e.g. life insurance premiums, are allocated directly to each member's accumulation account.

To continue with the example of Heather and Geoff, let's say in the 2014-15 financial year:

- Geoff's employer pays in contributions of $10,000 (concessional contribution) and Geoff personally contributes $30,000, where no tax deduction has been claimed (non-concessional contribution).

- Heather's employer pays in $5,000 (concessional contribution) and Heather personally contributes $15,000, where no tax deduction has been claimed (non-concessional contribution).

- The super fund earns interest of $8,000 and dividends from shares held by the super fund of $2,200. General expenses (administration fees, audit fees and ATO fees) amount to $3,800. Net earnings, therefore, are $6,400 ($8,000 + $2,200 - $3,800).

- Life insurance is paid for Heather at a cost to the super fund of $2,000 and for Geoff of $4,000.

- Income tax expense is calculated to be $60 [$6,400 (general net earnings) - $6,000 (life insurance premiums) X 15%]. For simplicity, I haven't included any franking credits in relation to the dividends received (defined in BPK#19).

At the end of 2014-15, the accumulation accounts of Heather and Geoff would look like this:

	Heather	Geoff	TOTAL
Opening Balance 1 July 2014	100,000.00	350,000.00	450,000.00
Percentage Split	22%	78%	100%
Add increases in members' accounts during the year			
Concessional Contributions **Taxed at 15%**	5,000.00	10,000.00	15,000.00
Non-concessional Contributions **Not Taxed**	15,000.00	30,000.00	45,000.00
Share of Net Earnings Heather - 22% Geoff - 78% **Taxed at 15%**	1,408.00	4,992.00	6,400.00
Less decreases in members' accounts during the year			
Contributions Tax of 15% (only applicable to concessional contributions). There would be no tax applicable to the non-concessional contributions Heather - $5,000 X 15% Geoff - $10,000 X 15%	(750.00)	(1,500.00)	(2,250.00)
Income Tax Expense of 15% (applicable to net earnings) =$60 Heather – 22% Geoff – 78%	(13.20)	(46.80)	(60.00)
Insurance Policy Premium Paid These costs are directly attributed to each member	(2,000.00)	(4,000.00)	(6,000.00)
MEMBERS' ACCOUNT BALANCE AS AT 30 JUNE 2015	**$118,644.80**	**$389,445.20**	**$509,090.00**
NEW PERCENTAGES FOR 2015-16 FINANCIAL YEAR	23%	76%	100%

The above would be included in each of the member's statements, as part of the preparation of the financial statements.

BPK#17 Using Reserves

In Chapter 3 I covered the use of contribution reserves (BPK#10) as they related to contributions to a self-managed super fund. There are other reserves which can be utilised which can include anti-detriment payments (covered in Chapter 13), investment fluctuation reserves, self-insurance reserves (covered in Chapter 10) and expense reserves. Investment fluctuation and expense reserves are like a contingency plan for your super fund to ensure that the liabilities of the fund can be paid as and when they fall due.

These reserves are funded by the investment earnings of the fund. Instead of the earnings being allocated to members they are allocated to the relevant reserve accounts.

There are of course the inevitable rules that relate to the operation of these reserves and the transfer out or allocation of the reserve funds. The main ones that you need to know are:

- The broken record rule – make sure your super fund's trust deed allows the fund to have the type of reserve your fund is contemplating

- There needs to be a separate investment strategy formulated for the proper management of each type of reserve and this should be consistent with the fund's main investment strategy

- Amounts transferred or allocated out of reserves are treated as concessional contributions, unless the amount is allocated in a fair and reasonable manner to every member, and is less than 5% of the value of the member's balance.

BPK#18 Capital Gains Tax

I'm not going to go into capital gains tax in great detail because it is a very complicated area and I could probably dedicate a whole book to it (what great bed time reading that would make).

The basic information that you really need to know is that when your super fund has an investment, covered in BPK#14, and the decision is made to sell it while you are in the **accumulation phase**, then if it has increased in value, your fund will have made a **capital gain** and you will have to pay **tax** on the profit that your super fund makes. This tax is referred to as capital gains tax and will apply to all investments when your super fund is in accumulation phase.

Capital gains tax is not applicable for those assets that are being used to fund any retirement benefits that are being paid by your super fund. This is related to the part of your super fund that is in pension mode.

If your super fund sells an investment and the amount your super fund receives from the sale is less than what it is valued in the records of your super fund, your super fund will make a **capital loss.** Your super fund cannot claim the loss. It can only offset the loss against a capital gain. So where this occurs, you will have to carry forward the loss until you can offset it against a capital gain. Your accountant will know how to account for this and what to include in your super fund tax return.

BPK#19 Franking Credits/Imputation Credits

I wanted to make special mention of franking credits, as this area will be relevant if your super fund has invested in Australian resident companies. I'll explain the advantages to your super fund of this type of investment.

The company that your super fund has invested in will pay tax on their earnings and then may issue a dividend to its shareholders. If you have a dividend statement from an Australian company, it will probably show the dividend paid and the **franking credit** or **imputation credit**, which is the tax paid by the company on behalf of you as the shareholder.

Your super fund has to show the amount of dividend actually received plus the franking/imputation credit on your super fund's tax return. It is included in the revenue part of the net earnings and 15% tax is paid on this. The advantage to your super fund is that your super fund can claim the entire franking credit/imputation credit against the tax. Let me illustrate:

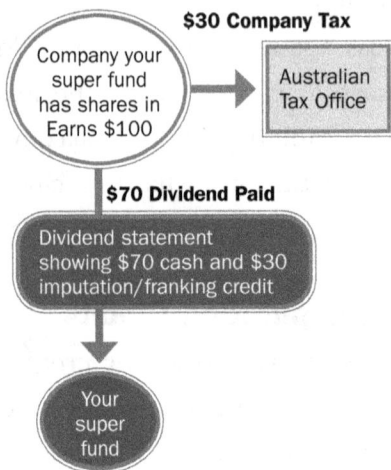

1. Say the net earnings of the super fund were $500.

2. The net earnings would include the $100 received from the company, i.e. cash received plus the imputation credit.

3. $75 tax would be payable by your super fund ($500 X15% tax rate), which includes $4.50 tax on the imputation/franking credit ($30 X 15% tax rate)

4. Your super fund can then claim the entire imputation/franking credit of $30, which reduces the tax that your super fund has to pay to $45 ($75 - $30).

To give another advantage: if you are over 60 and your super fund is in pension phase, your super fund does not pay tax, but the fund can still claim a reimbursement of the franking/imputation credits from the ATO through the super fund tax return.

Again, your accountant will know how to account for this and what to include in your tax return.

MANTRA
THERE'S A REASON THEY CALL IT A SELF-MANAGED SUPER FUND

You are the trustee of your super fund and *you* are ultimately responsible for your super fund. Not your accountant. Not your financial planner. Isn't that the best reason to take control? Just remember, with control comes responsibility.

Things you need to remember about the operation of your self-managed super fund

1. While you are still working, you are contributing to your super fund as a member, and this is known as the accumulation phase.

2. There is a variety of options your super fund can invest in.

3. Don't ever forget the sole purpose test, which dictates that your fund is maintained for the sole purpose of providing for your retirement, and not for satisfying your passion for boats, cars, art or wine. You, as trustee of your super fund, must ensure that any investment decisions are in line with the ultimate prize – enjoying your retirement to the fullest.

4. Tax is payable by your super fund in respect of some of the contributions, the net earnings and capital gains. The tax rate is only 15%, which is what makes self-managed super funds or any type of superannuation so attractive.

5. To take advantage of the low tax rate, your super fund has to be a complying fund, which means that your fund has to play by the rules.

6. As a member, your member's balance grows each year through contributions. Your balance is your share of the net earnings of the super

fund less any expenses directly attributable to
you as a member.

7. Your share of net earnings is based on the percentage of the total balance of your super fund
   that your balance represents.

8. If your super fund invests in an Australian resident company, this can mean franking or imputation credits, which can be claimed by your
   super fund, even after you are 60 and receiving
   a tax free pension.

CHAPTER 5

SHOW ME THE MONEY – HOW DO YOU ACCESS YOUR SELF-MANAGED SUPER FUND?

THE MOMENT YOU'VE been waiting for – "Show me the money!"

When can you access your super? How do you access it? How much can you access? And what about tax? These are the questions that I will answer in this chapter.

BPK#20 – When Can You Access Your Super?

To access your super, you must be over a certain age. This is known

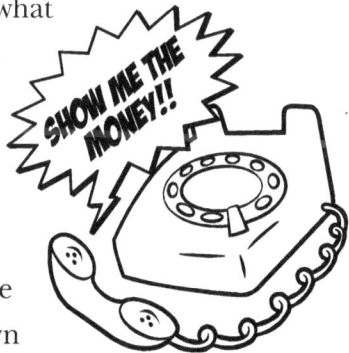

as your **preservation age.** At present, you can access your super any time after 55 to 60, depending on the year you were born.

If you have reached your **preservation age** or over and choose to access some of the benefits in your super fund, you will have met a **condition of release.**

When this happens, that part of your super fund that you are accessing, is classed as being in the **pension phase.**

You can also access your super if you meet the eligibility criteria for severe financial hardship, specified compassionate grounds (at present determined by the Commonwealth Department of Human Services), terminal medical condition or permanent incapacity.

BPK#21 – How Do You Access Your Super?

Lump Sum Or Annual Amount?

You have met a **condition of release** and want to access the benefits of your super fund. What happens then? There is no one rule dictating how your super fund will pay out the funds or benefit to you (surprise, surprise), as it depends on your age and whether you are still working.

Between Preservation Age (55-60) and 64

Presently, if you are between 55-60 and 64 and are still working, you can access your super through your super fund paying you what is called a **transition to retirement income stream**. This is income you receive at least once in a financial year and over successive financial years. There is a limit as to the amount that can be paid to you. You are not allowed to be paid the balance of your portion of your super fund as a lump sum.

The transition to retirement income stream amount you are paid is based on a percentage of the balance of your portion of your super fund. There is a minimum and maximum that you can be paid. At present the minimum is 4% and the maximum is 10%.

To illustrate – if the balance of your super fund is $750,000 and your share of the balance is $500,000, and your super fund is going to pay this entire balance to you as a **transition to retirement income stream**, then the minimum that you can be paid is $20,000 (4% of $500,000) per year and the maximum is $50,000 (10% of $500,000) per year. This means that your super fund can pay you anywhere between $20,000 and $50,000.

On the other hand, if between the your preservation age and 64 you decide that you don't want to work anymore and permanently retire, then you can nominate to receive a lump sum (any amount up to the balance of your portion of your super fund) or an income stream. This income stream is known as an **account based pension** and is like a **transition to retirement income stream** in that there is the same minimum amount that has to be paid (4% of your account balance at present). It differs in that there is no maximum percentage amount that needs to be paid.

As a trustee of your super fund, you need to ensure that you have a written declaration stating that you, as a member of your super fund, have no intention of working again for more than 10 hours a week.

Prorating

The annual income stream amount is based on 365 or 366 days and always covers the financial year period (1 July to 30 June). If your super fund starts paying an annual income stream after 1 July, the amount paid out will be less than the annual amount allowed because you are paying out over a lesser period. This is referred to as prorating the amount.

In the example above, if the annual income stream started on 1 September 2015, then the period that the income stream is being paid over is reduced by 62 days (July and August) from 365 to 303 days. The prorated minimum and maximum amounts would be:

Minimum (4%) $20,000/365x303 = $16,602.74 for the 2015-16 financial year.
Maximum (10%) $50,000/365X303 = $41,506.85 for the 2015-16 financial year.
For the 2016-17 financial year, the minimum and maximum amounts will then revert to being the full annual amounts of $20,000 (minimum) to $50,000 (maximum).

After 65

After 65, your super fund can pay you a lump sum or account based pension. The minimum amount will vary depending on your age, or how much older than 65 you are.

For example, at present, this minimum percentage for account based pensions ranges from 5%, if you are between 65 and 74, to 14%, if you are over 95. There is no maximum percentage and it doesn't matter if you continue to be employed.

Incapacitation, Terminal Illness or Financial Hardship

If you are permanently incapacitated or have a terminal illness, you can access your super on compassionate grounds and a lump sum can be paid out by your super fund. For cases of severe financial hardship, you can receive a limited lump sum (presently $10,000 in a 12 month period), if you are under **preservation age,** or an unlimited lump sum, if you are over preservation age. As usual, terms and conditions apply, so please speak to your financial planner or accountant if you need further information.

Annuity

Your super fund may also have purchased an **annuity** for you, which is done through an insurance company. When your super fund is in **accumulation phase**, it pays a lump sum or multiple amounts to the insurance company, and the insurance company invests these funds. Your super fund can nominate where these funds are invested. The annuity will keep building from the amounts that are being paid in by your super fund and also the annual earnings from what that money is being invested in.

When you meet a **condition of release**, the insurance company will pay you an annual amount each year. This can be a fixed amount (same each year); an indexed amount (increasing in line with inflation); or a variable amount (depending on what your lump sum has been invested in and the volatility and, hence, the return on those investments). An annuity is generally great if you want a bit of certainty.

Remember that your trust deed must allow for each of the different types of payments out of your super fund, so please check that it does.

BPK#22 – Accumulation And Pension Accounts

You can have multiple pension accounts but only one accumulation account

When you can access the money in your super fund, having satisfied a **condition of release** and chosen to do so, the balance of the fund that will be used to pay you a pension or income stream will be classified as being in **pension phase**. This will include the balance that will be paid out as a **transition to retirement income stream**. This balance of your super fund that is in pension phase is separately identified as a **pension account**, in contrast to your super fund's **accumulation account**.

You may choose not to have the entire portion of your balance of the super fund paid out as a pension or income stream.

You can still work when you receive a pension, which means you can still have contributions coming into your super fund (**concessional and non-concessional contributions**). These will still be going into your super fund's **accumulation account**.

Why is it important to separately identify the accumulation and pension accounts in your super fund? Well, when a pension is paid out as an income stream, there is a minimum percentage and possibly a maximum percentage that can be paid out. This is based on the part of your portion of the super fund balance that you want paid as a pension or income stream. So at the end of each financial year, there will be a balance that will be used to determine the next year's income stream. If you have all the funds lumped together, how will your super fund know what the annual amount is to be?

It is, therefore, possible to have more than one **pension account**. However, there will only ever be one **accumulation account**.

Not everyone may be in pension phase

In your super fund, there may be a member who is in pension phase at the same time another member is still in accumulation phase. As I have covered previously, there is no tax payable in relation to the pension account, including the earnings, but there is tax applicable in relation to the accumulation account.

These balances need to be separated, or **segregated**, to work out these tax free and taxable components for your super fund's tax return. In most self-managed super funds, they are not. This is referred to as the funds being **unsegregated.**

Where this is the case, that part of the balance of the super fund which relates to the pension phase needs to be worked out. This is known as the tax free or **exempt current pension income.** To work this out you, as trustee, will need to get an **actuarial certificate** from an **actuary.** An **actuary** will work out your super fund's **exempt current pension** income, which is always expressed as a percentage of your super fund's balance, and will provide your super fund with an **actuarial certificate** showing the percentage. This certificate is required annually in cases where you continue to pay a pension or income stream while your super fund assets are **unsegregated.** Your accountant will be able to arrange this for you, or you can just "Google" the term "actuary" to find one.

This will have taxation implications, which I cover in BPK#25.

BPK#23 – Starting And Stopping A Pension

After your super fund starts paying you a pension or income stream, it is possible to stop a pension account and "roll it back into accumulation." If your super fund does this, then the **pension account** will be added to the **accumulation account.** Your accountant or financial planner may recommend this on an annual basis so that you start a new pension at the start of the new financial year. They will recommend this action because of the great advantage of being in pension phase – no tax is paid on any earnings of the balance that makes up the **pension account.** This even covers circumstances where you sell one of the assets of your super fund that make up your **pension account** and your super fund makes a profit or capital gain. Normally, your super fund would be liable for capital gains tax, but because that part, or all, of your super fund is in pension phase, that applicable part that is in pension phase will not be liable for capital gains tax. How good is that?

But beware. Your pension phase could stop if your super fund doesn't abide by the rules for paying a pension or income stream, as outlined in the **Superannuation Industry (Supervision) Act 1993** and **Superannuation Industry (Supervision) Regulations 1994**. If, for example, it is not paying the minimum, or it is paying more than the maximum amounts, then your fund will no longer be classed as being in pension phase and will, therefore, not be able to take advantage of the zero tax rate. So you may have thought that you were in pension phase, sell an investment property for a profit, and expect your super fund is not liable for tax (capital gains tax). If, however, you have broken the rules, your super fund will have to pay the capital gains tax. How bad is that?

Naturally, a pension or income stream will stop when the balance of the pension fund is zero.

There's also the matter of a member receiving a pension or income stream dying. What happens then? I'll cover this area in Chapter 13, which is about planning for the inevitable and the unexpected.

BPK#24 – Trustee Responsibilities When Paying A Pension Or Income Stream

There are a few things that you'll need to be aware of, as trustee, when your super fund plans to start paying a pension or income stream.

Trust Deed

The biggie is the need for your trust deed to allow for the lump sum, type of pension or income stream that your super fund is proposing to pay. Make sure it does. If it doesn't, then you will need to arrange to have your trust deed changed before your super fund starts to pay out.

Application and Approval – Talking to Yourself

As a member of your super fund wishing to receive a lump sum, pension or income stream, you need to apply to the trustee of your super fund to have this happen. The trustee then needs to approve this application. A letter from the member to the trustee, even though it seems a bit weird to be writing to yourself, will suffice for the application, which should include the date you would like the pension to start, the amount of income that you would like to receive and how often you would like to receive it. For the approval process, minutes of a meeting recording the trustees approving the commencement of the pension will be required. As trustee, you will need to write to yourself, as the member, outlining the minimum payment requirements, the tax free amounts to be paid and any tax that will be withheld.

Revaluation of Assets

As trustee, before your super fund arranges to pay a pension or income stream, you have to arrange for the assets/investments of the super fund to be revalued. If you have a property, for example, you will need to arrange for a valuation. For shares, you will use the share price at that time. There may be a number of assets, so it will be necessary for you or your accountant to prepare a new set of financial statements to show the true financial position of your super fund at the time your super fund starts to go into pension phase. That way, you and the other trustees will have accurate figures from which to work out the minimum and maximum amounts that are applicable.

Product Disclosure Statement (PDS)

As trustee, you need to decide whether to issue a PDS. A PDS provides information on the benefits, risks, costs and fees associated with a financial product. A pension or income stream is classified as a financial product. (Refer to ASIC's Regulatory Guide 168 for more information.)

BPK#25 - What About Tax On Benefits?

Or, more importantly, why is tax payable?

A self-managed super fund lives in a low tax environment of 15% in relation to the concessional contributions being made and the earnings of your super fund. This continues whilst your super fund is in accumulation phase.

When benefits are paid out to you by your super fund, the government wants to ensure that you are personally paying the correct marginal rate of tax on those benefits. It does this by making your super fund collect the tax on their behalf and pay it to the ATO.

You, as trustee, are responsible for ensuring that any tax that should be withheld is and is then paid to the ATO. The tax to be withheld will depend on a couple of factors, the first being the proportion of taxable and tax free components that make up the balance that has been converted to a pension account and is being used to pay out the benefits. The second factor will be your age when your super fund pays out the benefit.

Taxable and Tax Free Components of Benefit Payments

In Chapter 4, I covered the **taxable** and **tax free** components of your accumulation account. These refer to whether the full marginal rate of tax has been paid (tax free component), or only the concessional rate of tax, or cases where no tax has been paid (taxable component) on those contributions and earnings.

Tax will be payable on the taxable component of the accumulation account when it converts to a pension account and benefits are to be paid. This will be applicable to benefit payments made to members up to 60 years of age.

No tax will be payable on the tax free components of your accumulation account when it is converted to a pension account and benefits are paid to you by your super fund.

So it is important, when your super fund balance is in accumulation phase, that these various components are calculated and recognised. There are resources available that assist in the calculation of these components, such as those available on the ATO website. Just make sure that your accountant is doing this for your super fund.

Your accountant will also be aware of the relevant tax rates that are applicable to the payment of an income stream or lump sum, depending on your age.

Deducting Tax from Benefit Payments

Once it has been determined that tax is payable, then, as trustee of your super fund, you are responsible for deducting or withholding the necessary tax and paying this to the ATO. To do this, your super fund needs to register with the ATO for **PAYG withholding tax**. When you deduct the tax from the payment to the member, you need to then pay this to the ATO.

At the end of the financial year, your super fund will then need to issue a payment summary (**PAYG Payment Summary**), which lists the payments made and the tax withheld. It is equivalent to the group certificate that you receive from your employer.

Proportioning Rule

Since there are taxable and tax free components of the super fund balance being used to fund the benefit payment, how do you know which component you are paying the benefit from and, therefore, how much tax needs to be withheld? The government has thought about that. There is a **proportioning rule** that means that whatever the tax free and taxable percentages are that make up the balance that is to be paid as a benefit, they will be the percentages that will be utilised to work out the taxable portion of the benefit payment. Let me illustrate:

Laurie, who is 56, has decided that he would like to continue working while receiving a transition to retirement pension from his self-managed super fund. He has an accumulation account with a balance of $500,000, which is made up of $300,000 (60%) taxable and $200,000 (40%) tax free components. He has decided that he would like to be paid 5% of the balance ($25,000) as an income stream. When the benefit is paid out, the proportioning rule dictates that $15,000 (60% X $25,000) will be taxable and $10,000 (40% X $25,000) will be tax free.

What do you do when you receive the benefits?

When you receive a PAYG Payment Summary from your super fund, you, as the member receiving the benefits, will need to include this information in your personal tax return.

Well, that was a big chapter. Hopefully, you're not suffering from information overload. My aim was to get you familiar with the terms and to simplify their meaning, so you know what to expect when your super fund goes into pension phase. That way, you'll know that your accountant or financial planner is doing it right. And you will be able to ask your accountant some questions with a degree of confidence.

MANTRA
THERE'S A REASON THEY CALL IT A SELF-MANAGED SUPER FUND

You are the trustee of your super fund and *you* are ultimately responsible for your super fund. Not your accountant. Not your financial planner. Isn't that the best reason to take control? Just remember, with control comes responsibility.

Things you need to remember about accessing your self-managed superfund

1. To access your super, you must be over a certain age. This is known as your preservation age.

2. If you have reached your preservation age, or over, and choose to access some of the benefits in your super fund, you will have met a condition of release.

3. When this happens, that part of your super fund that you are accessing, is classed as being in pension phase.

4. No tax is payable by your super fund in relation to the assets that make up the pension account, including the earnings.

5. There is no one rule dictating how your super fund will pay out the funds or benefits to you. It depends on your age and whether you are still working.

6. You, as a member of your super fund, can have multiple pension accounts but only one accumulation account.

7. Where there is a member in your super fund who is in pension phase and a member who is not, the funds will be referred to as being unsegregated. To work out the tax free or exempt current pension income that relates to the pension account, you, as trustee, will need to get an actuarial certificate from an actuary.

8. Once your super fund starts paying you a pension or income stream, it is possible to stop a pension account and "roll it back into accumulation."

9. Your trust deed needs to allow for the lump sum, type of pension or income stream that your super fund is proposing to pay.

10. There needs to be an application by you, as a member, to start a pension, and approval by you, as trustee, for this to occur – you need to talk to yourself. ☺☺

11. As trustee, before your super fund arranges to pay a pension or income stream, you have to arrange for the assets/investments of the super fund to be revalued. There also needs to be consideration of the issue of a PDS.

12. You, as trustee, are responsible for ensuring that any tax that should be withheld from a member who is receiving a benefit is and is paid to the ATO. Tax will be payable on the taxable component of the accumulation account, when it converts to a pension account and benefits are to be paid to any member under the age of 60.

13. Your super fund needs to register with the ATO for PAYG withholding tax. When you deduct the tax from the payment to the member, you need to then pay this to the ATO.

14. At the end of the financial year, your super fund will need to issue a payment summary (PAYG Payment Summary) to you, as a member. You need to include this in your personal tax return.

15. The proportioning rule dictates that the tax free and taxable percentages that make up the balance that is to be paid as a benefit will be the percentages utilised to work out the taxable portion of the benefit payment.

CHAPTER 6

IT'S TIME TO GO – WINDING UP A SELF-MANAGED SUPER FUND

THERE ARE MANY reasons why a self-managed super fund might be wound up. These include the following:

- You and all the other members of your super fund have realised that a self-managed super fund is not for you and you would rather be in a retail or industry fund.

- There has been a breakdown in the relationship between the members.

- There is nothing left in the super fund, as all benefits have been paid out.

- The cost to manage the fund is greater than the balance of the super fund.

- There are no members left in the super fund, as they have all passed away.

- A trustee has moved overseas and is no longer considered a resident for tax purposes, which is one of the requirements for being able to be in a super fund.

This chapter is about the simple "dos and don'ts" of the wind up process.

The most important thing to remember is that you, as trustee, have a responsibility to deal with the assets and members' benefits correctly.

THE DOS

- Check the trust deed, as this should have valuable information and rules for winding up the super fund.

- Make sure that there are minutes prepared and signed by each member and trustee of the super fund, agreeing to the wind-up.

- As trustee, obtain written advice from the members as to how they want their benefits paid out, i.e. rolled over into another super fund or paid out as a lump sum. For a lump sum payment, make sure that the member's benefit can be paid in this manner. They must satisfy a condition of release, which I talked about in Chapter 5 (BPK#20).

- Ensure that all reporting and compliance requirements for the previous financial year have been satisfied, i.e. preparation of financial statements, tax return, audit of the same and payment of all liabilities recognised in those documents.

- If all the assets of the fund are in cash, it will be relatively easy to pay out the benefits owing to the members. Where the assets are not, they may be able to be transferred as is (in-specie) or they may need to be sold so that benefits can be paid out to the members, or their beneficiaries, where the members have passed away. In the case of in-specie transfers, there may be capital gains tax implications, which need to be included in the financial statements. There will also be stamp duty implications for the member who is receiving the asset, because of the change of ownership. Because of these factors, including the possible costs involved, careful consideration should be given as to whether it would be better to sell the assets and then transfer the proceeds.

- Check with ATO regarding any monies owing to them.

- To determine an accurate picture of the net benefits that can be either transferred or paid out, organise the preparation of a draft set of financial statements. These will detail all the revenue and expenses of the fund to date and show the expected expenses to be incurred as a result of the wind-up. Don't forget to factor in any tax that will be payable.

- Once all trustees are satisfied that there is an accurate financial picture, ensure all transfers or payouts of members' benefits are affected correctly.

- Prepare a final set of financial statements and arrange for an audit to be conducted.

- Lodge the final income tax return.

- Finalise any payments that need to be made to the ATO.

- Notify the ATO within 28 days of the super fund being wound up. The ATO will cancel the ABN of the super fund, officially close the fund and advise all trustees that they have closed the super fund.

- It is important that all revenues (including tax refunds from franking/imputation credits, where the fund is paying tax exempt income streams) and expenses are calculated and included in the statements. Just be sure that, if required, there is enough cash to pay for expenses post wind-up, as this will mean that your super fund will not have to prepare another set of financial statements, and tax return, and have them audited.

- Where there is a corporate trustee, a decision has to be made whether to keep the company going or to deregister it. If it keeps going, there will be ongoing administrative costs.

DON'TS

- Don't immediately close the bank account – once you have closed it, it can't be reopened unless there is a new trust deed. You need to ensure that all payments to the ATO, and anybody else that needs to be paid, have been made first.

- Don't cancel the ABN. The ATO will do that for you once you formally advise them that your super fund has been wound up.

- Don't get rid of any of the super fund's documents and records. It is required that these be kept for a period of 5 years. Any trustee declarations require keeping for 10 years.

MANTRA
THERE'S A REASON THEY CALL IT A SELF-MANAGED SUPER FUND

You are the trustee of your super fund and *you* are ultimately responsible for your super fund. Not your accountant. Not your financial planner. Isn't that the best reason to take control? Just remember, with control comes responsibility.

Things you need to remember about winding up

1. Check the super fund's trust deed for guidance.

2. Minute all action.

3. Where the assets of the super fund are not in the form of cash and can't be readily transferred, sell them to realise cash.

4. Get an accurate picture of the financial position of the fund before transferring or paying out to members.

5. Ensure transfers or payouts are effected in accordance with legislation and the fund's trust deed.

6. Prepare the final financial statements and tax return and arrange for them to be audited.

7. Lodge the final tax return.

8. Pay the ATO what the super fund owes them.

9. Notify the ATO of the wind-up.

10. Ensure the super fund has enough money to pay any expenses post wind-up.

11. If a corporate trustee, decide whether the company needs to be deregistered.

12. Don't immediately cancel the bank account and don't cancel the ABN.

13. Keep all records and documentation in relation to the fund.

CHAPTER 7

TO BORROW OR NOT TO BORROW? THAT IS THE QUESTION

I WANTED TO WRITE a separate chapter on borrowing because this is an aspect of having a self-managed super fund that has a lot of appeal. So much of that appeal appears to stem from being allowed to have real estate as part of the investments of your super fund. The lure of having that investment unit at the beach or, if you are in business, being able to buy a commercial property to operate your business out of, is very strong.

So do you want the good news or the bad news? Okay, I'll start with the good news – yes, your self-managed super fund can borrow to buy property; this has been allowed since 2007. But the bad news? The bad news is that there are a few hoops that you have to jump through first. What is the proper process? What are the rules? And what do you really need to consider, including the risks? This is what I will cover in this chapter. That way you can decide if it's really worth it from a time and cost perspective.

The **Superannuation Industry (Supervision) Act 1993** directly prohibits self-managed super funds from borrowing. Of course, like so many other rules in the wonderful world of self-managed super funds, there are exceptions. One of these exceptions is borrowing to buy property through, wait for it, a **limited recourse borrowing arrangement or LRBA**. Yes, one of those terms that makes you just want to switch off and say it's all too hard, so I'll try and explain it so it doesn't seem that bad.

If, as trustee, you decide that your super fund would like to invest in property, which, for most super funds, would be real estate or shares, there may be a need or want to borrow in order to do it. The first thing that you, as trustee of your super fund, need to ensure is that your super fund's **trust deed** allows your super fund to borrow.

Borrowing to buy property and shares has to be a strategy that you, as trustee, have determined will help you to achieve that **sole purpose** of being able to provide for your retirement. This needs to be reflected in your **investment strategy**, which is a formal planning document that your super fund must have. I cover this in more depth in Chapter 9.

Given that this is probably a major investment for your super fund, minutes should be prepared to document the decision. This ensures that all trustees of your super fund are in agreement with this particular course of action.

To best illustrate the next steps, let's assume that your super fund is going to invest, through borrowing, in property. You, as trustee of your super fund, have had a look around and found something suitable.

THE PROCESS

Step 1 – Talk to your lender

The first step is to talk to your lender, probably your bank, and seek pre-approval for the loan. It's no use going through the next costly and time-consuming steps in the process if the bank is not willing to lend your super fund the money.

Banks are very cautious when it comes to lending to a self-managed super fund. As with any form of lending, they will want to ensure that repayments will be made on the loan. In the unlikely event that something goes wrong and they need to repossess the asset, they want to make sure that they are not going to make a loss in the process. They will, therefore, want your super fund to contribute a percentage of the value of the property and will lend the super fund the remaining percentage. This is known as the **loan-to-value ratio.** It is no different to borrowing to buy your own home, where the bank wants you to contribute a minimum of, say, 20% towards the purchase price of the property. At the moment, the loan-to-value ratio for LRBAs is lower than that for residential property lending, which means that your super fund has to contribute more of the purchase price.

If the lender is willing to lend 65% (**loan-to-value ratio**) of the value of the property, your super fund has to contribute 35% of the purchase price.

In relation to this LRBA process it is okay for your super fund to borrow from anyone including a related party. I cover this point in a bit more detail later in the chapter.

Step 2 – Set up a separate entity to hold the property in trust, a bare trust

So let's assume that your super fund can contribute the necessary percentage and the bank will lend to your super fund. Given that a self-managed super fund can't borrow, except through an LRBA, the **Superannuation Industry (Supervision) Act 1993** requires that your super fund set up a separate entity outside the super fund to buy and hold the asset. This separate entity is always another trust, as it is only holding the property in trust for your super fund.

Just like your self-managed super fund, this separate trust will have one or more trustees. The trustee/s in this separate trust can't be the same as the trustee/s for your super fund. So if you are the individual trustee of your super fund, you can't be the trustee for this separate trust. Similarly, if you have a company (corporate trustee) as trustee of your super fund, that company can't be corporate trustee of this separate trust. This is because, under trust law, you can't hold property on behalf of yourself.

This separate trust is called a **bare trust,** or **security trust,** because it can barely do anything but hold the property in trust (on behalf) of your self-managed super fund.

The trust deed should note that the trustee of the bare trust will transfer ownership of the property to your super fund once the loan has been repaid.

Minutes of both your super fund and the bare trust should reflect and approve all the actions being undertaken by the parties and between the parties.

Your super fund is responsible for paying any deposits, repaying the loan, receiving the income and paying any expenses associated with maintaining the property.

Your self-managed super fund is the **beneficiary** of the bare trust, as your super fund will eventually gain ownership of the property (see, there is a happy ending). So, visually, this is the structure:

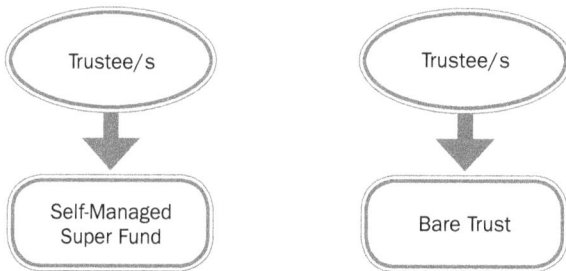

The bare trust will have a trust deed, which, as for your self-managed super fund, will set out what it can and can't do. It should, of course, revolve solely around the holding of the property on behalf of your super fund. The bare trust will have no discretion in relation to dealing with the property. The bare trustees cannot, therefore, sell the property.

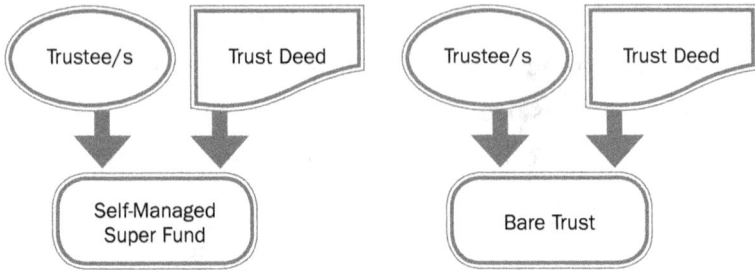

Step 3 – Sign a contract to purchase the property

A contract to purchase the property is signed. This has to be in the name of the bare trustee, as the bare trust is the legal owner of the property until the loan is repaid. Your super fund, as the beneficiary and therefore the beneficial owner of the property, pays the deposit.

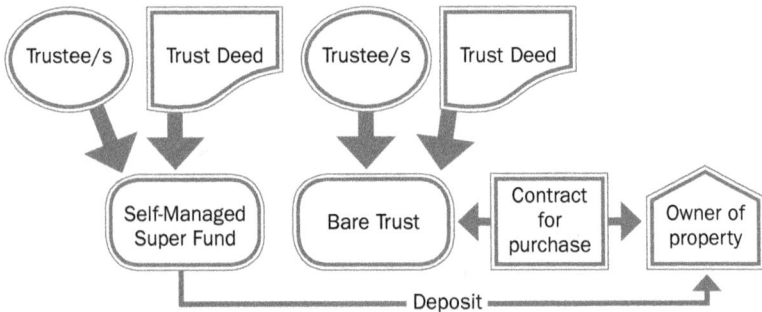

Step 4 – Finalise the loan

As trustee of your super fund, you will then go to your lender and finalise the loan. The loan is between your super fund and the lender. The bare trust will have legal ownership of the property and your super fund will have beneficial ownership. As I said previously, because of the trust deed, the bare trust can't do anything with the property but hold it in trust for your super fund until your super fund gains ownership.

The loan agreement should include that it is a **Limited Recourse Borrowing Arrangement (LRBA)**. This means that, should your super fund not be able to repay the loan, then the only action (recourse) that the lender can take is to repossess the asset that the borrowing relates to. They can't touch anything else in your super fund. So if the property is sold and there is a shortfall between the sale proceeds and the amount owing on the loan, your super fund does not have to pay money to cover the shortfall. That is why the banks will insist on a lower **loan-to-value ratio**.

Banks may also insist on a personal guarantee from you, as trustee, and the other trustees of your super fund. This means that if there is a shortfall between the sale proceeds and the amount owing, they can make you honour that shortfall.

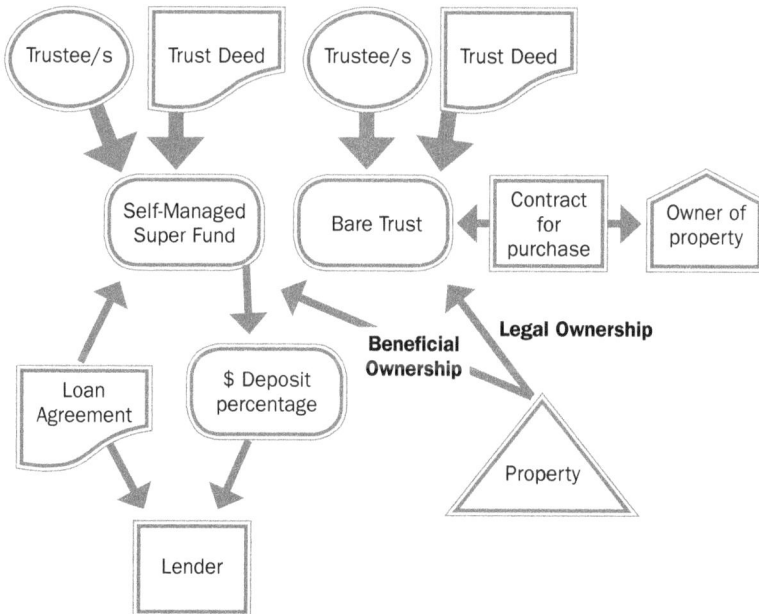

Step 5 – Have the bare trust deed stamped

Given that the property is an investment property, when it is sold or transferred, there could well be capital gains tax implications. There is also stamp duty that needs to be paid. To minimise this, your super fund needs to have the fact that the property is being held in trust officially recognised. This is done through going to the relevant state government authority, e.g. Office of State Revenue in Queensland, and having it acknowledged by them on the bare trust deed. This is known as having the trust deed stamped, because that is literally what happens. This should happen after the loan has been approved and after settlement of the purchase has occurred. This could save your super fund a lot of money.

Repayments will be made by your super fund. As mentioned previously, it is your super fund that will collect and account for any income, as well as being responsible for any expenses.

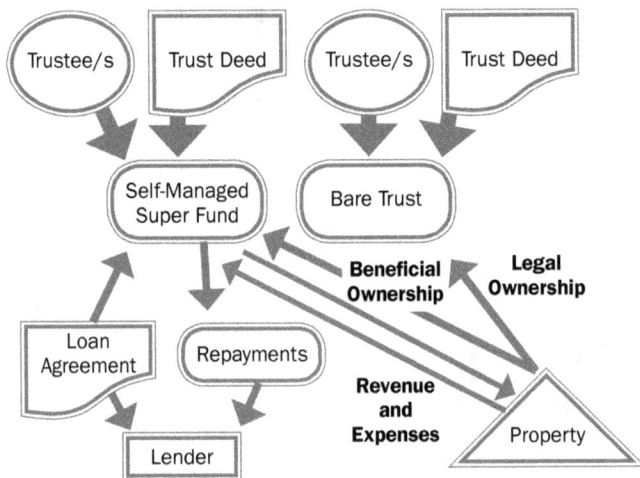

Step 6 – Transfer ownership when loan is repaid

Once the loan is repaid the bare trust will still have legal ownership of the property because the original contract is in the bare trust's name. The property and the legal ownership will then be transferred from the bare trust to your super fund - the happy ending.

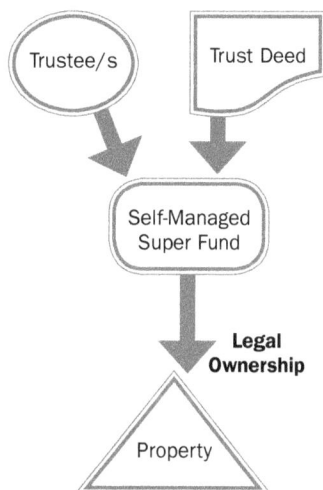

We've covered the **process** that needs to be followed, so now for some of the rules that you should be aware of. I'll cover what kinds of property your super fund can purchase through borrowing; what your super fund can do after the initial purchase and borrowing process; and related party borrowings.

THE RULES

What can you purchase?

The first important question you probably want answered is: **"What kind of property can your super fund purchase through borrowing? "**

Your super fund can purchase what is referred to as a **single acquirable asset**, which, as the name suggests, means one asset. That could be land, a land and house package or a parcel of shares in one company, but it has to be classed as one asset. This can be restrictive and it can get complicated. Let me give you a couple of examples to illustrate:

1. Property sitting over two titles – this may or may not be okay, depending on whether the titles could be sold or dealt with separately (not okay) or if there is some law that says they can't be dealt with separately (which is okay).

2. Buying an investment unit and a car space – this would not be okay if there were separate titles. It would be okay if there weren't separate titles.

What can you do after you purchase?

After your super fund has purchased the property, there are rules in the **Superannuation Industry (Supervision) Act 1993** about what you can and can't do while your super fund has a borrowing in place. The golden rule is that once your super fund has purchased the property, money can be spent on repairing and maintaining it, but money can't be spent on significantly improving it to the point that the essential character of the property is changed. That sounds fairly straightforward, but it isn't. I will provide you with some examples, which are by no means exhaustive, but give you an idea of what sort of minefield your super fund is entering when you, as trustee, decide to borrow to buy property.

These are some of the things that your super fund **cannot** do whilst it has a borrowing in place:

IT CAN'T

* Have more than one borrowing under a bare trust arrangement. If your super fund wants to borrow to buy further properties, then your super fund has to arrange for another bare trust to be set up.

* Borrow more than once in relation to a particular asset.

* Use some of the borrowings to improve the asset (it *can* use some of the borrowings to repair or maintain the property).

* Buy a block of land and then build on it. Your super fund can't improve or change the character of what your super fund purchased.

* Buy the worst house on the best street and then do major renovations to the house.

* Buy a block of land and then sub-divide it.

* If your super fund has a house and it burns down, it cannot be replaced with a block of units.

* Buy a property and build a pool in the back yard or build a garage and driveway.

✖ Buy a house and then make alterations so that it
   is then being used to operate a doctors surgery
   or other type of commercial business.

I could now go on and give you examples of the difference between repairs and maintenance and improve-
ments, but it is so open to interpretation that it could take
up another chapter. I just want to bring home to you that it
is not straightforward, so be really, really careful if you are
considering making any changes once your super fund has
purchased the property. It's a fine line between being right
and being wrong, and the consequences could really affect
the type of retirement you enjoy.

If you are in this situation and, as trustee of your super
fund, want to do some major work on a property that your
super fund has a borrowing on, I really would recommend
that you seek advice from your accountant or your auditor
as to how they would view it from a compliance perspective.

Buying from a related party

The same rules that apply to the transferring in of assets
(**in-specie contributions**) apply here. Your super fund can't
buy property from a **related party**, with the exception of
commercial property and listed shares. If you do purchase
commercial property or listed shares from a related party,
remember that it must be at market value.

Who can you borrow from?

With a LRBA, your super fund can borrow money from anyone. This could mean a bank, another financial institution or a **related party** to your super fund. So even you, as a member, can lend to your super fund for this purpose. If you do lend to your super fund, you must ensure all the dealings in relation to that loan are at **arm's length**, or, in other words, undertaken in the same manner they would be if a bank or other financial institution were lending to your super fund. There needs to be a proper loan agreement in place, including, amongst other things, the property details, the borrowing amount, the interest rate and the term of the loan. Most importantly, it would need to reflect that this loan is a LRBA.

THE GOOD, THE BAD AND THE UGLY

Last, but not least, comes **the good, the bad and the ugly section** of this chapter. It's about what's great about borrowing, what's not so great and what the risks are.

The Good

Borrowing to buy property is a great, low tax alternative to otherwise buying property, personally or even through a company. Any net income is taxed at only 15%, if your super fund is in accumulation phase, or zero if the property is supporting the payment of an income stream from your super fund in the pension phase. If you held it personally, it would be taxed at your marginal rate of tax, or at the company rate of tax if held through a company, both of which would be higher than 15%.

The Bad

There are inevitable costs, both in terms of time and money, involved in setting up the separate company structure for the bare trust, producing the trust deed and other administrative requirements. Banks may also charge extra in the loan application because they will have to look at all the various trust deeds and other documentation to ensure that everything has been put in place correctly. They will want to check that there will be minimal risk for them in the event that your super fund defaults on the loan and they have to repossess the property.

Another downside is that any equity that your super fund has in the property can't be used to borrow to buy further properties, either inside or outside your super fund.

The Ugly

Your super fund has to make the repayments on the loan, so you need to be confident, as trustee, that your super fund will be able to do that. There are not only loan repayments, there are also the other expenses that have to be met. And you need to be able to maintain the income stream from the property. What if you can't rent the property out? Is there enough cash in your super fund to keep paying the loan? Your super fund's ability to repay the loan is one of the factors that the bank or lender will look at when considering your super fund's loan application.

Another risk is in relation to the **loan-to-value ratio**, which is the percentage of the value of the asset that the bank is willing to lend. In the case of your super fund borrowing to purchase shares, because of the risk of volatility in the share market, the bank will probably include a clause in the loan agreement about margin calls. This clause effectively means that if the price of the shares drops to a level where the loan-to-value ratio is not being maintained, then the bank can make a margin call and force your super fund to pay money in to restore the loan-to-value ratio.

But coming in at number one of the BIG, BIG risks of borrowing is the fact that, if your super fund breaks any of the rules, then it may be required to sell the property. This could be at a substantial loss and, because your super fund has contravened the law, it could be liable to penalties. Imagine what that would do to your super fund balance?

Remember the sole purpose test

As you can see, this area is complicated. It's so hard to try and simplify it. On reflection, I think that I could write a whole book just on borrowing by self-managed super funds.

I hope you are still awake.

This has by no means been the A-Z of borrowing by self-managed super funds, but I hope you have learned enough to be cautious. You are now better equipped to ensure that the correct process is followed and your super fund is complying with the legislation.

The last words that I have for you on the subject? Never, never lose sight of the **sole purpose test**. Your super fund must be maintained for the sole purpose of providing for your retirement. Make sure borrowing fits in with that philosophy. I'd really like to see you having the best retirement you could hope for.

MANTRA
THERE'S A REASON THEY CALL IT A SELF-MANAGED SUPER FUND

You are the trustee of your super fund and *you* are ultimately responsible for your super fund. Not your accountant. Not your financial planner. Isn't that the best reason to take control? Just remember, with control comes responsibility.

Things you need to remember about borrowing

1. Your super fund can borrow under a **limited recourse borrowing arrangement** or **LRBA**.

2. It's called an LRBA because the action (recourse) available to the lender is limited to repossessing the property and they can't take anything else in your super fund.

3. Ensure your super fund's trust deed and investment strategy allows your fund to borrow.

4. Ensure all decisions and actions are documented in minutes of your super fund.

5. Talk to your lender first to seek pre-approval for the loan.

6. A separate trust fund called a **bare trust** has to be set up to buy and hold the asset on behalf of your super fund, though it has no discretion in dealing with the property.

7. A bare trust will have its own trust deed outlining that it holds the asset in trust and that it will transfer ownership to your super fund when the loan is repaid. It should also minute all decisions and actions taken.

8. The trustees of the bare trust must be different from the trustees of your super fund.

9. Your super fund is the beneficiary of the bare trust and will gain ownership of the property when the loan is paid off.

10. Your super fund is responsible for all costs associated with purchasing and maintaining the property and will also receive any income from the property.

11. The contract for the purchase of the property has to be in the name of the bare trust.

12. When the property purchase settles, the bare trust deed should be stamped to indicate that the property is being held in trust for the super fund, as this minimises capital gains or stamp duty issues when the property is transferred.

13. The property is transferred from the bare trust to your super fund on repayment of the loan.

14. Your super fund can only purchase a **single acquirable asset**.

15. Your super fund can't purchase property from a related party, with the exception of commercial property and listed shares.

16. Once purchased, your super fund can only maintain or repair the property and cannot significantly improve the property, i.e. cannot significantly change the character of the property.

17. Your super fund can borrow from a related party but this must be on an arm's length basis.

18. Borrowing is a great low tax alternative to buying property personally or through a company.

19. There are costs both in terms of time and money involved in your super fund borrowing.

20. As trustee, make sure that your super fund can make the repayments on the loan and meet the other expenses associated with maintaining the property.

21. The rules create a minefield. It is an extremely complex area and the BIG, BIG downside, or risk? If you break the rules, your super fund may need to sell the property and will be liable for penalties. What will that mean for your retirement?

CHAPTER 8

RISK – DIFFERENT STROKES FOR DIFFERENT FOLKS

BECAUSE YOUR SUPER fund embodies your life savings and you know how precious it is, the two biggest fears you probably have in relation to superannuation are the questions: "Will I have enough?" and, "What happens if I lose a big part or even all of my super fund?"

Uncertainty fuels the fears that we have. It will drive your risk appetite and, therefore, the risks that you are willing to take. There is risk in anything that we do and this is never truer than when we invest in a self-managed super fund.

Hence, in this chapter, I want to talk about all things risk – different risk appetites; why these exist; and how your attitude to risk affects your decisions, as trustee, regarding what your super fund invests in. I also want to address the biggest risk of all, which is actually having a self-managed super fund to begin with.

For those of you who have a self-managed super fund, this chapter will probably come across as a combination of me stating the bleeding obvious and you learning a little more. For those of you who are thinking of investing in a self-managed super fund, hopefully, reading this chapter will provide important food for thought.

I'm going to touch on the top five risks that you need to consider. These can greatly affect how well or how badly your super fund performs and, in the end, how much you have to enjoy in your retirement.

1. The first big risk factor is return on your investment, or being greedy. The rule of thumb here? Generally, the higher the return, the higher the risk. Higher returns, of course, mean that the balance of your super fund will grow quickly. But they also indicate that there is a higher risk that something can go wrong with your investment. You could lose some, or even all, of those precious life savings. Just look at what happened during the global financial crisis.

Here's a prime example of the relationship between risk and return. On the one hand, you could invest some of your super in cash, by having a bank account or investing in a term deposit, which is low risk/low return.

Compare that with investing in the next best thing that comes along, such as ostrich farms or olive grove investment schemes.

Here, investors can make spectacular rates of return, but there is a big risk of those returns not being realised. Ostrich farms and olive trees were very fashionable a few years ago. They are more of a fad type of investment. It amazes me that they still appear to operate despite the bad publicity these types of schemes have had over the years. There was a case as recently as December 2013 in which the collapse of a Queensland olive grove investment scheme meant investors lost more than $39million. There is a class action being taken against the financial advisors involved. Hopefully, the failed investors may see the return of some of their investment, but they face the prospect of losing their entire life savings. You could easily become one of these people, as there is nothing to stop you, as trustee of your super fund, from investing in schemes such as these.

The good news is that there has been a decline in the number of opportunities to invest in ostrich farms and olive groves. The bad news is that there is always something equally as risky waiting to replace them. There's always the next best thing.

If you are being offered high rates of return, don't be greedy. I would strongly recommend that you think about what you are investing in. What exactly do you know about the opportunity you are considering? Why are you being offered such high rates of return? The answer to that, of course, is risk. You need to fully explore what those risks are. Do your research. "Google" like crazy for anything that will give you information about the down side of the investment. As they say – if it sounds too good to be true, it probably is. You need to make a fully informed decision, not one that is totally dependent on what your financial advisor is telling you. If it all goes pear shaped, can you go and live with your financial advisor when you retire? Will they feed and clothe you? Remember the mantra: ***You*** **are the trustee of your super fund and** ***you*** **are ultimately responsible for your super fund. Not your accountant. Not your financial planner.**

2. The second big risk factor is your age. The older you are, the more conservative you become, and can probably afford to be, because you will have accumulated a healthy balance in your super fund. When you are younger, you are still trying to build the balance in your super fund. The more years you have until retirement mean the more risks you will be likely to take regarding how and where you, as trustee, invest your super fund.

Coupled with this is how much you have thought about superannuation over the years and how healthy your super fund is. If you have a balance in your self-managed super fund of, say, $250,000 and are 45, you will no doubt have a higher risk appetite than if you are the same age and have a balance in your self-managed super fund of $750,000. It's all driven by a strong desire to provide for a healthy retirement.

3. The third big risk factor is putting all your eggs in one basket. By this I mean investing all your money in only one type of investment. Property is a prime example and appears to be on the "must have" list of investments for a self-managed super fund. Don't buy an investment property just because it's a nice "have." Yes, it can be a great investment, but only if you can afford it and it is earning your super fund money. Are you getting a decent rate of return on your investment? This is even more important if your super fund borrows to buy the property. How will the super fund make loan repayments? What about the ongoing bills and what happens if you can't rent it out? You, or any related parties, can't rent or live in it yourself. Remember the rules. You can't enjoy it until you retire (**in-house rules**) and you need to meet the **sole purpose test** that your super fund is there for the sole purpose of providing benefits for your retirement. If it is costing more than it earns to have this investment in your super fund, what is happening to the balance of you super fund?

I have heard some horror stories. Like the couple close to retirement, not with a large balance in their super fund, being advised to purchase an investment property and borrow money to fund it. How will they continue to make repayments when they retire and are no longer contributing to their super fund? Will the rent cover the repayments? This is one of the prime examples where you could hear those fateful words, "Holy crap! Where's my super gone?"

Diversification is one of the most important things to consider. Spread your investments around. The larger the balance you have in your super fund, the better the opportunity to be able to diversify.

4. The fourth big risk factor is failing to plan. Failing to plan can be the equivalent of planning to fail. As trustee, you need to consider all the above risks and actually plan out what you need to do about them. What do you want at the end of this journey to retirement? How much money do you want to have as your little pot of gold at the end of the rainbow? What kind of risk appetite do you need to have to achieve that? I have only one word for you here – PLAN. This is absolutely essential. Don't be like those ostriches in those ostrich farm investment schemes and bury your head in the sand, hoping like hell that you will reach retirement age and have it magically happen.

Life doesn't work like that. You have to have a plan. In a self-managed super fund, this comes in the form of the little-appreciated **investment strategy.** This I will cover in more depth in the next chapter. It gets a whole chapter to itself – that's how important this document is.

5. The final risk is the risk of actually having a self-managed super fund. You really need to consider whether it is worth it from both a cost and time perspective.

There are many costs involved, which you probably found out after the fact. This is probably one of your biggest gripes about having a self-managed super fund. These costs include:

- The cost of setting up the fund, and, possibly, setting up a company, if you have a corporate trustee;

- Management fees, including paying an advisor, such as a financial planner, who monitors your super fund and advises you accordingly;

- Investment fees, if your super fund is investing in a managed fund;

- Administration and accounting fees;

- Audit fees;

- ATO fees or levies; and

- Legal costs.

These costs can eat away at the earnings of your super fund and mean that you will not build your retirement fund as quickly as you might like. The cost of running a self-managed super fund can be expressed as a percentage of your fund balance. To give you an idea, at present, for nearly two thirds of self-managed super funds, this percentage is 1% (a statistic straight from the ATO).

You will find, however, that the larger your balance, the lower this percentage will be. This is because there are fixed costs such as audit fees, ATO levy and accounting fees, which are spread over a larger balance and, hence, result in a smaller percentage.

So what is the rule of thumb for the correct amount you should have before you invest in a self-managed super fund? I am asked that question often and there are many and varied opinions on it. I think the best way to provide you with an indicative answer is to quote a 2012 study undertaken by Rice Warner, which was commissioned by the Australian Security and Investments Corporation (ASIC). ASIC are the body that oversees advisors, auditors and those that provide products and services to self-managed super funds. The purpose of the study was to examine the minimum cost-effective balance for self-managed super funds compared with APRA regulated superannuation funds (mainstream retail and industry super funds). Rice Warner concluded:

- **Less than $100,000** Self-managed super funds are not as competitive as APRA-regulated funds unless they are expected to grow to a competitive size within a reasonable time.

- **$100,000 to $200,000** Can be competitive with more expensive APRA-regulated funds if the trustees undertake the broader investment and administration

- **$200,000 to $500,000** Can provide equivalent value with APRA-regulated funds provided the trustees undertake some of the administration.

- **$500,000 or more** Can provide equivalent value to APRA-regulated funds on a full service basis (i.e. trustees rely solely on their financial advisors).

So, as you can see, there is not a definitive answer, but it does give you an idea. And it really advocates that if you want a cost effective self-managed super fund, you need to be quite actively involved. That will mean time. Can you afford to take the time? In my opinion, you can't afford not to. This is your life savings we are talking about. This is about enjoying retirement to the fullest. In other words – remember the mantra.

MANTRA
THERE'S A REASON THEY CALL IT A SELF-MANAGED SUPER FUND

You are the trustee of your super fund and *you* are ultimately responsible for your super fund. Not your accountant. Not your financial planner. Isn't that the best reason to take control? Just remember, with control comes responsibility.

Things you need to remember about risk

1. The higher the return, the higher the risk – don't be greedy.

2. The more years you have until retirement, the more risks you are likely to take regarding how and where you, as trustee, invest your super fund.

3. Don't put all your eggs in one basket – diversify.

4. Failing to plan can mean you are planning to fail.

5. You need to consider whether having a self-managed super fund is worth it from a cost and time perspective.

CHAPTER 9

GOT TO HAVE A PLAN, STAN

WHILE IT IS fresh in your mind, I want to talk about the all-important planning that we touched upon in the last chapter. Remember, failing to plan can be the equivalent to planning to fail.

Never lose sight of the **sole purpose test** of having an SMSF. The sole purpose is to provide funds for retirement, servicing the ultimate goal of being able to enjoy your retirement to the fullest. What is your super fund investing in at the moment? Is it helping you achieve that precious goal?

It's great having that control and being able to determine how you will invest your super funds. And it's great having the opportunity to invest in things that wouldn't be possible in an APRA regulated fund. But how do you know, at the end of it, whether you will be able to sit back and completely relax in retirement?

The answer to that is planning. Actually write down what you want in the end and how you are going to achieve it. This method is applicable for all aspects of your life. There are many, many books written on how to achieve success and most of them centre around having long term goals. Where do you want your life to be in, say, three years and how are you going to get there? You can then break that down further into annual goals. You could have all of this swirling about in your head but all it will do there is swirl about. The really important thing here is to write it down. There's nothing like having a visual reminding yourself of what your goals are.

Setting goals and having a plan are a fantastic start but they only go half way. The action that goes hand-in-hand with having a plan is to keep reviewing it to check that you are on track and also to see if it needs to change. Once a year, as part of your annual goal setting, you should reflect on what has happened in that past year and what have you achieved. Then, in order to progress towards your three-year goal, determine what you want to action in the coming year. And don't forget the very important point of writing it down.

Managing your self-managed super fund should be no different, and you, as trustee, should plan for both the short term and the long term. The government sees this planning process as being vital. So much so, it has made it compulsory that trustees of self-managed super funds have to document a plan, or **investment strategy**, which needs to be reviewed annually. The reality that I see first-hand, when I audit self-managed super funds, is that trustees pay lip service to this necessity. They will even ask me if I have a template or an example of an investment strategy that they can use so that they are satisfying legislative requirements. Accepting "Here's one that I prepared earlier" is one of the worst disservices you could do to your financial future. I suggest that you embrace the planning and reviewing process.

What should you look at as part of your investment strategy? There is plenty of guidance. Where better to look than the legislation itself? The **Superannuation Industry (Supervision) Regulations 1994** actually set out the minimum items that you need to consider when formulating your investment strategy. I think they really do provide a great checklist. The five items that you, as trustee, have to think about as a minimum consideration for planning for the future are:

1. **Risk** – we covered risk in the last chapter. What is important to say here is that you need to write down the risks associated with the investments you, as trustee, are proposing for your super fund, or those your super fund has already invested in.

2. **Returns** – remember, usually, the higher the risk the greater the return.

3. **Diversification** – look at whether the investments will provide your super fund with the necessary funds for your retirement. Make the projections and do the math. It's all about risk and controlling that risk, as we saw in the last chapter. On the whole, the more you can diversify your super fund's investments, the lower the risk. Also, the lower the balance of a super fund, the less chance you have to diversify and the greater the risk.

4. **Liquidity** – this is about considering the cash flow needed for your super fund. How liquid are the fund's investments? In other words, how easily and quickly can your fund's investments be converted to cash? If you have invested in property, this is not a very liquid asset. And if you have low cash reserves or few assets that you could quickly turn into cash, what happens if the super fund has to pay expenses or a pension but doesn't have the money? This is a very important aspect to think about and one of those not properly considered by trustees of self-managed super funds. People get star struck by the variety of what their super fund can invest in and, instead of being objective, indulge their passion for fast cars, fancy boats or even fancier wine. Stay objective and always plan to have the money to pay your super fund bills and benefits (pensions, income streams) when needed.

5. **Insurance for members –** this is contingency planning and such an important aspect of the planning process. It addresses the "What if?" that I'll discuss further in the next chapter.

These are the minimum requirements and I would treat them as such. Put as much time and effort into this process as you can. And don't, whatever you do, just let your trusted advisors do it for you. Work with them, but be sure *you* understand and control the process.

Don't just write it down – really embrace it. Rather than having a look at it annually, have a look at it every three months. Put pictures in your investment strategy – pictures of exotic places that you want to visit, of the boat or the investment unit down the coast that you will finally get to enjoy, the wine, the paintings. Make it the mother of all plans and treat it with the respect and importance that it deserves.

You may not be in this alone. Where there are other members in your super fund, every member needs to be involved in the planning process. You need to consider the biases of other members regarding what they would like the super fund to invest in, as well as their risk tolerance.

Don't just look at it from an annual perspective either. Look long term. Start with how much you want to have in retirement – what is your pot of gold? Do the math – make the projections. What do you need to have along the way to achieve your goal? Seek advice from your financial planner. This is their bread and butter stuff – a good financial planner eats investment strategies for breakfast. They are a very important part of your team when it comes to achieving your retirement goal.

If you consider all these factors, then you will increase your chances of maximising your retirement benefits. Create your own investment strategy. One size does not fit all. Think about the factors that we have talked about in this chapter and consider your individual circumstances.

MANTRA
THERE'S A REASON THEY CALL IT A SELF-MANAGED SUPER FUND

You are the trustee of your super fund and *you* are ultimately responsible for your super fund. Not your accountant. Not your financial planner. Isn't that the best reason to take control? Just remember, with control comes responsibility.

Things you need to remember about planning

1. Planning is all about the ultimate goal of being able to enjoy your retirement to the fullest.

2. It's mandatory to have a plan, or investment strategy, for your super fund and to review it annually.

3. The five things that you need to have thought about as a minimum, and have included in the investment strategy for your super fund, are: risk, returns, diversification, liquidity and consideration of insurance for members.

4. Really embrace the planning process and treat it with the respect and importance that it deserves.

5. Put pictures in your investment strategy.

6. Rather than having a look at your investment strategy annually, have a look at it every three months.

7. Every member of the super fund needs to be involved in the planning process.

8. Think long term and seek advice from your financial planner.

CHAPTER 10

INSURANCE – HAVE YOU REALLY THOUGHT ABOUT IT?

Guess what? You're not covered

As with your super fund's investment strategy, I don't think that people who have self-managed super funds understand the importance of insurance. This is definitely reflected in the disturbing statistic that in 2010-11 only 25% of self-managed super funds chose to hold insurance (*ATO Self-managed super funds: A statistical overview 2010-11*).

Why is this disturbing? Well, if you are in an APRA regulated superannuation fund (retail or industry main stream fund), you have a certain level of insurance coverage, the cost of which is built into the fees you pay. Switch to a self-managed super fund and you lose those insurance benefits.

Like the mandatory investment strategy, the government saw it being equally as important that trustees of self-managed super funds consider insurance for the members of their fund. They made it compulsory under the **Superannuation Industry (Supervision) Regulations 1994** that insurance for members should be considered. So while it's not compulsory for your super fund to have insurance for the members, what *is* compulsory is that you, as trustee, should *consider* it. This consideration *must* be undertaken. It could be documented in the minutes of your super fund but should also definitely be part of your documented **investment strategy.**

I've seen, so many times, a one-liner in the investment strategy saying it has been considered, purely for the purpose of paying lip service to this legislative requirement. As trustee of your super fund, you need to really think about this aspect of managing your super fund, and not just consider it as something that you have to show compliance with.

Why aren't you insuring?

Think about what will happen if you die, become terminally ill, you can't work, you are injured or you suffer some sort of medical trauma. Depending on where your super fund is in its life cycle, these events may cause not only emotional upheaval, but may also threaten the financial stability of your super fund. This would especially be the case if you are still well and truly in the **accumulation phase** and have debt in your super fund. The above circumstances would severely affect the ability to continue to contribute to your super fund and therefore the ability of your super fund to service debt and pay other expenses.

So if your financial advisor has not discussed insurance with you, or even mentioned it, if they've not debated your particular circumstances so that you can give it due consideration, then I suggest that they are doing you a disservice.

What kind of insurance to have?

What kind and what amount of insurance should your super fund consider? The insurances that *could* be considered are life, total and permanent disability (TPD), trauma and income protection (temporary incapacity).

There are numerous experts in the field recommending against having insurance coverage in your super fund in relation to trauma and income protection.

The government has recognised this also. From 1 July 2014, it is not possible to have trauma insurance in your super fund. They have also narrowed the type of TPD insurance that a super fund can have to "any occupation" and have excluded "own occupation". "Own Occupation" insurance covered what you did in your current job whereas "any occupation" would mean you couldn't be employed in any occupation. It is still possible to keep this kind of insurance coverage post 1 July 2014, if you had insurance already in place at that date. For the purposes of this chapter I will therefore only cover life, "any occupation" TPD insurance and income protection.

In the case of income protection (temporary incapacity) insurance, although your super fund can claim the premiums as a tax deduction, you can personally claim the premiums on your tax if you pay for them yourself and, given that your marginal rate of tax is probably higher, it makes more sense for *you* to have the deduction rather than your super fund.

There is a significant downside to having TPD insurance in your super fund, as tax is payable on the payout (dependent on your years of service and how close you are to retirement). It is tax free, however, if the policy is held completely outside super.

You should, therefore, still consider TPD (any occupation) and income protection insurance but it's probably better to do that outside of your super fund sphere.

It is very much, as I mentioned, a case of looking at your individual circumstances, e.g. if you are retired, receiving a pension, have a healthy super balance and little or no debt, then it is highly unlikely that you would want or need insurance. The general rule is that the greater the debt you have in your super fund, the younger you are and the greater the income you are earning, the greater the amount of insurance you will need to consider.

Insurance can, of course, be expensive, which affects your ability to maximise your retirement benefit. If you do have insurance inside your super fund, then it is an expense of the fund, which will lessen the fund balance and, therefore, the payment of retirement benefits.

Your super fund is always the owner of any policy that it takes out for the members, so always make sure that policies are made out in the name of the trustee of the super fund.

Cost of Insurance

The cost of insurance can be so expensive as to be prohibitive. Your super fund does not have the same purchasing power as an APRA regulated fund. One option to consider, as well as having your self-managed super fund, is to join an APRA regulated fund that provides life insurance at a reasonable cost and have some of your contributions directed to the APRA regulated fund. You would need to look at the costs associated with this, e.g. administration costs, to determine if this is a cost effective alternative.

Self-Insuring

Some super funds have self-insured by quarantining some of the funds into a reserve in case any members have an accident. This is now prohibited (from 1 July 2013) and if funds are self-insuring they will only be able to do this until 30 June 2016.

What happens when there is a payout?

If a payout is received from a policy, the proceeds will be paid into your super fund. Your fund is the owner of the policy and you, as trustee, will need to ensure that any payouts to members or to dependents (from life insurance) are made in accordance with the law.

The first factor to consider is that there must be a **condition of release** before there can be a payment of the proceeds, as this is another form of benefit being paid from your super fund. From 1 July 2014, a condition of release, may be death, terminal illness, total and permanent incapacity (any occupation) or temporary incapacity.

In the cases of income protection (temporary incapacity), terminal illness (part of life insurance policy) or total and permanent incapacity (any occupation), the payout would be paid by the trustee of the super fund directly to the member.

In the case of a payout from a life insurance policy on the death of a member, the trustee of the super fund decides on the **beneficiaries** of the payout. The payout would, however, need to be in accordance with any instructions that the member may have given to the trustee. This is usually in the form of a **Binding Death Nomination.** This is formal, written and witnessed advice to the trustee, which needs to be renewed every three years (Lapsing Binding Death Nomination) or is permanent (Non Lapsing Binding Death Nomination). I cover this in more detail in Chapter 13.

As in the case of all strategies in your super fund, please be sure that your trust deed covers insurance and the strategy that you, as trustee of your self-managed super fund, are proposing.

This chapter gives you the basics you should be aware of in order to make more informed decisions about insurance and have more of a meaningful conversation with your financial advisor.

MANTRA
THERE'S A REASON THEY CALL IT A SELF-MANAGED SUPER FUND

You **are the trustee of your super fund and** *you* **are ultimately responsible for your super fund. Not your accountant. Not your financial planner. Isn't that the best reason to take control? Just remember, with control comes responsibility.**

Things you need to remember about insurance

1. If you are in an APRA regulated superannuation fund (retail or industry main stream fund), you have a certain level of insurance coverage. Switch to a self-managed super fund and you don't.

2. It's not compulsory for your super fund to have insurance for the members. What *is* compulsory is that you, as trustee, should *consider* it.

3. This has to be part of your documented investment strategy.

4. Why are you insuring? To cover circumstances that will severely affect your ability to continue to contribute to your super fund and, therefore, the ability of your super fund to service debt and pay other expenses.

5. What kind and what amount of insurance should your super fund consider? The types of insurance that can be considered, from 1 July 2014,

are life, terminal illness (part of life insurance), total and permanent incapacity (any occupation) and income protection (temporary incapacity).

6. The general rule is that the greater the debt you have in your super fund, the younger you are and the greater the income you are earning, the greater the amount of insurance you will need to consider.

7. Don't under-insure and don't over-insure – it may be more than your super fund can afford.

8. The cost of insurance can be so expensive as to be prohibitive, so consider joining an APRA regulated fund that provides life insurance at a reasonable cost and have some of your contributions directed to the APRA regulated fund.

9. Your super fund is always the owner of any policy that it takes out for its members, so always make sure that policies are made out in the name of the trustee of the super fund.

10. A condition of release must be met before there can be a payment of a benefit as a result of a payout from an insurance policy. A condition of release may be death, terminal illness, total and permanent disablement (any occupation) or temporary incapacity.

11. As in the case of all strategies in your super fund, please be sure that your trust deed covers insurance and the strategy that you, as trustee of your self-managed super fund, are proposing.

CHAPTER 11

BAD ADVICE – A WHOLE WORLD OF PAIN

As you are aware, Australia operates under a compulsory superannuation contribution environment where, if you are earning over a certain amount (presently $450 a month) and between 18 and 70, your employer has to contribute a percentage of your salary or wages to a superannuation fund.

With the APRA regulated superannuation funds, you have a limited degree of control over where your funds are invested, as that is managed on your behalf. They do give you choices in the form of ready-made options, usually based on your attitude to risk or, more likely, on how close you are to retirement. These options are given exotic titles such as "moderate," "accelerated growth" or "socially responsible."

Alternatively, you can choose a combination of what you want to invest in, such as cash, bonds and shares.

What a great opportunity... But then there's the risk

As you have read, self-managed super funds offer a greater opportunity to exercise the right of choice and control, and can be very effective in maximising your retirement dollars. In the wrong hands, however, they can just mean high risk. A friend of mine, who is an accountant and business coach, summed it up pretty well. When I told him that I was writing a book on self-managed super funds, and especially a chapter on risk, his reaction was to say, "I'd be putting in images of ticking time bombs, hand grenades and terrorists lurking around the corner – I don't think enough people are aware that they are playing with their retirement funding and this comes without a safety net." That sounds scary, I know, and this is an aspect that you are probably blissfully unaware of. Having the knowledge, however, can reduce the risk of that time bomb going off.

Seeking advice should be an integral part of your super fund strategy. But if this advice ends up being bad advice, the consequences can be devastating. Just ask those people who had their self-managed super funds invested in failed investment companies such as Opes Prime, Storm Financial, Wickham Securities and Trio Capital. Just to give you an idea, in the case of Trio Capital, it collapsed $123 million in debt and affected 288 self-managed super funds. I know first-hand of another friend of mine, Alison, who, along with her husband, invested their self-managed super fund dollars with Wickham Securities. Of course, they lost the lot. Alison is the one who suggested the title for my book; there's no doubting how *she* feels on the subject.

The Australian Securities & Investments Commission (ASIC), which regulates the advisors in the self-managed super fund space, has also been concerned about the advice being provided. They wanted to gain an understanding of what was happening and what especially the problem areas were in this sector. They set up the inevitable task force in 2012 and the end result was *ASIC Report 337 SMSF's: Improving the Quality of Advice Given to Investors,* which was published in April 2013. I'm telling you about this report because I think it gives an invaluable insight into the world of advice in the self-managed super fund sector and also gives a great summary of what you should be aware of when trying to protect your super fund. In this chapter, I share some of the report findings along with issues I have found from my own experience.

Make sure your advisor is licenced

The first important point is to ensure that anyone who is providing advice to you is licensed. *Providing advice* covers any situation in which someone is suggesting to you what to do with your money. This includes an advisor actually recommending that you set up a self-managed super fund in the first place, as well as advising what your super fund should invest in. Those providing advice have to hold an Australian Financial Services licence. You can check by searching ASIC's online public register of AFS licensees or authorised representatives.

Be aware of what your super fund doesn't have access to

In the last chapter, you discovered that a self-managed super fund does not have the insurance coverage you would in an APRA regulated super fund, so you need to consider it as part of your investment strategy.

Another fact that you should be aware of is that, unlike APRA regulated funds, self-managed super funds do not have access to a compensation scheme and are not entitled to receive compensation in the event of theft or fraud. Has your advisor let you know about that? I wonder when the self-managed super fund investors in some of the high profile collapses found out?

Self-managed super fund members also do not have access to the Superannuation Complaints Tribunal to resolve complaints, a forum that is available to APRA regulated funds. If you are having issues with your advisors, it is up to you, as trustee, to sort them out. This can involve a lot of time and money in costly legal battles. Licensed advisors should be members of an ASIC approved external dispute resolution scheme, which investors may have access to. It's a good idea to check if your advisor has maintained membership.

What does bad advice look like?

Some of the examples of bad advice that were highlighted in ASIC Report 337, and some that have cropped up in my own experience, are worth sharing with you to highlight the ugly side of advice:

- The starting balance of the self-managed super fund is so low that the costs of managing and maintaining the super fund will come to more than the super fund is earning. The balance is only going to go one way. The advisors do not raise this as an issue.

- Suitable alternatives to a self-managed super fund are not considered or discussed with the client.

- Advisors don't consider the long-term planning objectives of the clients and whether a self-managed super fund meets those objectives.

- Investors are approaching pension phase and their advisor recommends investing in a super fund. This is despite the fact that the fixed costs of running the super fund mean the fund balance will diminish while paying a pension.

- Advice is given to invest in a self-managed super fund even though the client wants a low maintenance superannuation solution or can't handle their own finances. This is a very important point – if you can't handle your own personal finances, how are you going to control and manage a self-managed super fund?

- A couple nearing retirement is advised to buy a property in their self-managed super fund. What if they can't get a tenant? How are they going to service the debt?

- The trustees of a self-managed super fund are advised to buy a commercial property, which becomes the major asset of the super fund. Little cash is left over. The members of the super fund, who have a business, rent the commercial property from the super fund at a commercial rate. What if the business goes bad?

- Investors are advised that it is okay to use a self-managed super fund to gain early access to superannuation savings. It's definitely not okay.

- An advisor recommends that you invest in companies or property developments that they are involved in or associated with. Ask the question, because that is a conflict of interest and would be completely unprofessional. A prime example of this was in the case of Wickham Securities, where investors' funds were invested in other companies that the chairman was involved in.

Beware those property spruikers

I want to make special mention of property spruikers, or those who extol the virtues of your self- managed super fund investing in property. I've mentioned property a few times throughout this book. Self-managed super funds have been allowed to invest in property since 2007 and they have embraced this opportunity with gusto. As I've said previously, I think this is in part because of Australians' love affair with property ownership. I am not saying don't invest in property – it can indeed be a valuable addition to your investment portfolio. All I am cautioning is to be careful of those snake oil salesman out there.

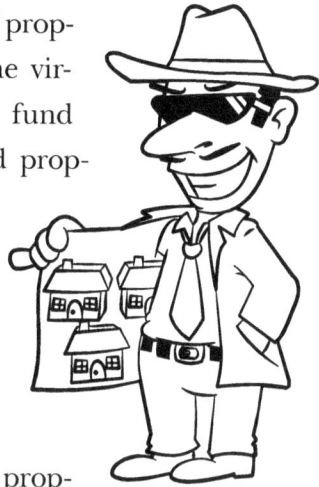

Some property spruikers will make claims of fantastic returns. A prime example of what is popular at the moment is investing in residential properties through the National Rental Affordability Scheme (NRAS), which is a federal government scheme aimed at providing affordable housing. There are payments and tax incentives offered for building and leasing properties to low and moderate income earners at 20% below the market rate. Property spruikers encourage self-managed super funds to purchase a property using the scheme and receive "$100,000 tax free." Wow – how great is that? And on the face of it, it *is* great. What lies below the surface, however, is what they don't tell you:

- To be in the scheme, you have to purchase 100 or more properties before you become an approved participant;

- When your self-managed super fund purchases an NRAS property, your super fund is purchasing from the approved participant – *they* will be the one gaining the fabulous incentives;

- There is no rule that says they have to pass on the incentives to you;

- There are probably fees associated with purchasing, tenanting and managing properties purchased from NRAS-approved participants;

- To receive that fabulous, financial incentive of $100,000, your super fund needs to be in the scheme for 10 years. Will your approved participant still be in the industry in 10 years? Can you hold your breath that long?

- In the meantime, your super fund will be required to rent out the NRAS property at 20% below the market value to eligible tenants. Is that the kind of return on your investment that you want? Think of the effect that will have on your super fund balance.

This kind of investment doesn't sound so fabulous now, does it? ASIC were so concerned about this type of investment that they issued a media statement in October 2013 outlining the above concerns. I also note that the federal government Department of Social Services (DSS), responsible for the running of the scheme, also felt compelled to put the following warning on their web page related to NRAS:

> It has been brought to the Department's attention that there have been some instances where individuals are being approached by people claiming to be representatives of the government with regard to investing in a property under the NRAS Scheme.
>
> In response, DSS notes that the government does not authorise or register individuals or organisations to speak to members of the public about NRAS investment.
>
> In particular, DSS officers do not:
>
> - contact members of the public promoting NRAS;
>
> - seek to make appointments with people at their home; or
>
> - contact members of the public asking for personal information, such as banking details.
>
> If approached in this manner, we recommend that you do not give out any personal information, such as banking details, and if you are uncomfortable with the nature of the call or approach, just hang up.
>
> *If you have already provided information to the individual or individuals and you are concerned that a crime has or may be committed, contact the police.*

Now, there's some food for thought.

What is the government doing about the bad guys?

So what is ASIC, the regulator, doing to prevent or deter these and other unscrupulous operators in the industry? ASIC has many big sticks it can use, which vary from injunctions and civil penalties to seeking criminal charges and banning orders.

ASIC took enforcement action against the directors of Trio Capital, their investment manager, a number of financial planners who recommended Trio and Trio's auditors. In the case of Wickham Securities, ASIC were successful in obtaining court orders to freeze assets, banning Bradley Sherwin, the chairperson of Wickham Securities, from providing financial advice, and also banning the auditor. This court case is proceeding now.

I have not yet read of any action being taken against property spruikers, but it is probably early days yet.

It is great to hear some action is being taken but, for those people who invested their self-managed super fund dollars in these failed companies, it probably won't bring those their precious life savings back. It really is better to be safe than sorry.

Some of the bad things that can happen you won't have any control over, like theft or fraud. In issues where you *can* have control, however, what can you, as trustee of your super fund, do to try and combat bad advice? One of the first things is what you are doing right now – finding out what the basics of a self-managed super fund are, what your responsibilities are, and taking those responsibilities and control of your self-managed super fund seriously. Remember the mantra and ask the right questions.

The next important step is to keep asking those questions until you get the right answers. If you don't understand the answer, it's not that you are not intelligent enough; it's just a case of it not having been explained well enough to you. Keep asking until you understand.

If you have a self-managed super fund, reflect on the examples that I have given you in this chapter and throughout the book and see if any ring true for you. If they do, what do you need to do about it? Do you need to ask more questions of your financial advisor/s or do you need to get another opinion, like you would for a serious medical problem? Maybe you need to take your super fund as seriously as your health – they both affect your future.

MANTRA
THERE'S A REASON THEY CALL IT A
SELF-MANAGED SUPER FUND

You are the trustee of your super fund and *you* are ultimately responsible for your super fund. Not your accountant. Not your financial planner. Isn't that the best reason to take control? Just remember, with control comes responsibility.

Things you need to remember about seeking advice

1. Self-managed super funds offer a greater opportunity to exercise the right of choice and

control and can be very effective in maximising your retirement dollars. In the wrong hands, however, they can just mean high risk.

2. Self-managed super funds do not have access to a compensation scheme and are, therefore, not entitled to receive compensation in the event of theft or fraud.

3. Self-managed super fund members also do not have access to the Superannuation Complaints Tribunal to resolve complaints. If your super fund has issues with your advisor it could involve a lot of time and money in costly legal battles.

4. There are plenty of examples of bad advice. These have been highlighted in ASIC Report 337 and in my own experience.

5. Be careful of those property spruikers. I am not saying don't invest in property – it can indeed be a valuable addition to your investment port-folio. All I am cautioning is to be careful of those snake oil salesmen out there.

6. ASIC has many big sticks it can use, which vary from injunctions and civil penalties to seeking criminal charges and banning orders against those offering bad advice.

7. For those people who invested their self-man-aged super fund dollars in failed companies,

their precious life savings probably aren't coming back. So it really is better to be safe than sorry.

8. To combat the bad advice, find out what the basics of a self-managed super fund are, what your responsibilities are, and take those responsibilities and control of your self-managed super fund seriously.

9. Ask questions and keep asking those questions until you get the right answers. If you don't understand the answer, keep asking until you do understand.

CHAPTER 12

COMPLIANCE – THE ELUSIVE AUDITOR

WE DON'T ONLY COME OUT AT NIGHT

THE ALL-IMPORTANT CHAPTER – it's all about me. I knew if I put in a chapter about audit at the beginning of the book, you would never have kept reading the book. So now that I have lulled you into a false sense of security, here it is.

"God, how boring is this chapter going to be?" I can practically hear you thinking. When people ask me what I do, I tell them I'm an auditor and I feel the need to justify to them that I'm really not that boring. You probably think auditors are those people, devoid of personality, who sit in their dimly lit offices wearing sensible cardigans with patches on the elbows. Their calculators click away and they love nothing better than finding something wrong.

When they do find some-thing, they smile and, with a flourish of their green pen, proudly docu-ment what your indiscre-tion is. In your mind, we probably look something like the lady on the right.

Having been in the industry for many years, I have met plenty of auditors and for some of them, the above pretty well describes them to a tee. I bet most of you have never met the auditor of your super fund, have you? I even had a client say that very thing to me just recently and their financial advisor, who was at the same meeting, said, "Yes, she only comes out at night."

You also probably haven't been that interested because the audit of your super fund is one of those mandatory things that you have to have done – we're your necessary evil. I totally get that, but I put it in the class of *you don't know what you don't know*.

Your involvement with your audit and auditor may currently be confined to signing the required **Trustee Representation Letter**. This is another document you probably dutifully signed where the "sign here" sticker was. This is a letter provided to your super fund auditor as part of the annual audit. This letter makes representations in relation to:

- Sole purpose test
- Trustees' status (not disqualified)
- Trust deed, trustees' responsibilities and fund conduct
- Investment strategy
- Accounting policies
- Fund books and records
- Fraud, error and non-compliance
- Asset compliance and valuation
- Uncorrected misstatements
- Ownership and pledging of assets
- Related parties
- Borrowings
- Subsequent events
- Outstanding legal action
- Going concern
- Any other additional matters that you, as trustee, consider that your auditor should be aware of.

But signing a Trustee Representation Letter at the time of your audit is not your only concern, as trustee of your super fund, when it comes to having an audit completed.

That's why I am writing a whole chapter about audit. Because this is one of the important reasons I actually wrote this book. This is where I can get up on my soap box and let you know how important your auditor and audit are for the well-being of your super fund. Auditors are more than your necessary evil. To know us is to love us and, hopefully, by the end of the chapter, you'll be wondering where we've been all your life.

The two main risks I see in the audit of your super fund are the risk of cheap audits and the risk of independence. These are the risks I think you, as trustee of your super fund, should be aware of.

There should be no such thing as a $300 audit

Since I started auditing self-managed super funds, something that has concerned me is how little people can and are willing to pay to have the audit of their super fund done. Practices were offering to do an audit for a flat fee of $275 a couple of years ago and, since then, it has marginally increased to about $300. I've also seen an ad where a firm will do the setup of your super fund and all your administration and compliance work in the first year for free. Would you do that with your job? "Yes, I'll work for you for the first year free. No need to pay me." It doesn't make sense.

I'm not the only one who is concerned. I attend technical conferences and training sessions on audits of self-managed super funds (I know, I need to get out more) and this is a continuing concern I hear from all of the auditors who attend these sessions. "How can anyone do an audit that cheap?" is a refrain I hear constantly (the ones who *are* doing the cheap audits aren't attending those conferences or technical update sessions, so don't answer). I think the question, though, is: "How can anyone do an audit **properly** that cheap?"

Why would we be wondering that? Because there's a huge amount of amount of training and experience that auditors have to gain to even qualify to audit your self-managed super fund. To give you an idea, I have to be registered with the Australian Securities and Investments Commission (ASIC), which is a requirement that came into effect on 1 July 2013. To achieve that registration, I had to have an accounting degree, which took me three years; I had to be a Certified Practising Accountant (CPA), which took me another three years; and then I had to gain the relevant experience in performing and signing off on audits of self-managed super funds, which was over a minimum of a one year period. So I have had to undertake a minimum of seven years' experience to be able to gain my registration and audit your self-managed super fund. That is the equivalent study required to be a solicitor, barrister or a doctor.

Then there is the ongoing training. To call myself a CPA and also keep my self-managed super fund auditor registration, I have to satisfy continuing professional development requirements, which is why I attend those riveting technical conferences. So, as you can see, I have had to and I continue to expend a lot of time and money on being a self-managed super fund auditor. Lucky I'm so passionate about it.

So your auditor has the qualifications and training, but what is involved in the audit of a self-managed super fund? Your accountant prepares a set of financial statements and tax return and your auditor has to check the figures in the financial statements and tax return to make sure they are accurate. This is Part A of the audit. Your auditor also has to ensure that you are complying with the **Superannuation Industry (Supervision) Act 1993** and **Superannuation Industry (Supervision) Regulations 1994.** There are 29 sections or regulations that your auditor needs to ensure that your super fund is complying with. This is Part B of the audit. An audit report is then issued in which your auditor gives separate opinions on Part A and Part B. In relation to Part B, if your super fund has not complied with any of those 29 sections or regulations, depending on the severity, your auditor is required to report these contraventions to the Australian Tax Office.

To perform the audit of your self-managed super fund properly, the minimum time that I could take on an audit would be 4-5 hours – and that's for a super fund with minimal diversification of investments. That could be the case if everything were there and there were no issues. Unfortunately, I've yet to come across one where that's been the case. Gosh, it would be boring if it all went that smoothly. So when it comes to charging $300 to do an audit – do you think that a doctor or a solicitor would provide an equivalent service for that price? I doubt it. So how do they do it? Are they performing a thorough enough audit?

If you are paying peanuts to have your audit done, guess who will probably be doing it? I haven't seen too many monkeys getting their university degrees.

Oh, and by the way (just in case you also don't get out enough), I have included a summary of those 29 sections or regulations at Appendix B to give you an idea of what your auditor looks for, or should be looking for, when they audit your super fund. Are there any of these aspects that you know you are not complying with? If so, why hasn't your auditor discussed any of them with you?

One of the ways that your auditor could be doing your audit so cheaply is through outsourcing. They might even be outsourcing your audit overseas. I have heard of some ridiculously cheap prices for having an audit done off shore, which is all to do with what the wage rates are in places like the Philippines. Do you know whether your audit is being outsourced to somewhere outside of Australia? Would you be comfortable with your information going overseas? Remember, this information includes your bank account details, as bank statements and other sensitive financial information are made available to your super fund auditor.

So what are you risking in settling for a cheap audit? You are risking your fund not complying with the rules because someone has done a quick *tick and flick* and missed issues of non-compliance. So what? What's the worst that can happen? Well, if the ATO do an audit of your super fund and find issues, then you may be up for increased taxes and fines, which could wipe out half or more of your super fund balance. Examples of some of the big taxes that you will pay are:

- Where income that is earned by your super fund is from a related party (non-arm's length) – taxed at 45%

- Where a member's tax file number has not been provided for the contributions being accepted by the super fund – taxed at 46.5%

- Concessional contributions above the concessional cap – taxed at 46.5%

Can you imagine how that will affect your retirement? There goes sipping that dry martini whilst sitting around the pool on the luxury cruise you have been dreaming of. As I have stressed previously, do you think it is your accountant or your auditor who will have to pay the additional taxes? No, No, No – it's your super fund that will pay the cost.

Your auditor needs to be independent

Another thing that you really should consider is the independence of your auditor. As I said at the beginning of the chapter, I see this as being a big risk to your super fund. If you are like the majority of self-managed super fund trustees, you just let your accountant handle that side of things and they arrange the audit of your self-managed super fund for you. In some cases, this can mean the administration, accounting and audit are all being done by the same accounting firm. The ATO, who regulate the auditors of self-managed super funds, have a big concern about this independence issue. So much so that the rules for accountants, including auditors, in relation to this issue have been beefed up recently. Accounting firms who do provide this one-stop-shop service justify it by saying that the audit division is separate from the accounting services division. In the industry we call these Chinese walls. But the fact remains that the accountant preparing the financials and tax return and the accountant who is auditing your super fund are still both working for the same firm and that has the ability to affect their independence. Independence is so important to ensure that you achieve a completely objective audit and audit opinion on the compliance of your super fund. Remember the possible consequences.

So ask the question of your accountant – who do they get to perform the audit of your super fund? Is it done in-house?

My take on audit

Have I convinced you yet of how important the quality and independence of the audit process is? I hope so.

Here's how I see audit. I definitely don't see it as being what I term a *tick and flick* process. I really enjoy working with my clients to get it right; I don't work with them with the aim of crucifying them if they don't.

I was once offered a bundle of 4,500 audits from an accountant who wanted a quote, which I gave him. He told me it was too high. He was having them done for $250 a fund no matter the size. He told me that his current auditor was now too busy to do them. I, of course, wondered why. I said

165

that I could not do the audits for that price, even though I had done the sums in my head and the total earning figure from doing 4,500 audits for $250 seemed very attractive – that was a lot of zeros. He told me they were easy and all that would be required was a *tick and flick* audit. I told him that I didn't do *tick and flick*. I could have outsourced them to the Philippines, sure, but why would I? Just to make a quick dollar? No way. Needless to say, I didn't add 4,500 audits to my practice. What concerns me most is the quality of the service provided by that accountant. What are they willing to accept on behalf of their clients? I would be questioning any professional who was willing to put my super fund and my retirement at risk.

Along with your financial planner and accountant, the auditor of your super fund should be an integral part of your super fund team. They are the gatekeeper and safekeeper of your super fund. There is a difference between your auditor and your other advisors. Financial planners advise you on the best way to manage your money and plan for your financial future. Any advice that they provide should be while adhering to legislative requirements. Accountants can also advise you on planning for your financial future, as well as accounting for what is happening with your finances. They produce your super fund financial statements and tax return and should also be ensuring that your super fund is complying with legislative requirements. But your auditors are advisors in that they advise whether you actually *are* adhering to legislative requirements, so it is a very different but important role they play.

Accountants who provide services to self-managed super funds also offer accounting services in a lot of different industries so are probably not solely concentrating on self-managed super funds. It is a complex environment so it is all the more important that you have an independent source like your auditor to confirm that your super fund is getting it right. That's the way you will be able to enjoy your retirement to the fullest.

My advice to you is not to accept being part of the sausage factory of cheap audits. Don't be one of the 4,500 audits or one of the audits that are outsourced overseas. Get to know your auditor and make sure you feel comfortable with them. Ask them questions. Make sure they are independent. Your auditor should be happy to speak to you all year round to ensure you and your other advisors are getting it right. That way there won't be any nasty surprises when audit time comes around.

Hopefully, you've now got a whole newfound appreciation for your auditor and why they are so important. You should not settle for second best just for the sake of ticking the box to say you've met legislative requirements. Never lose sight of the all-important goal of enjoying your retirement to the fullest.

MANTRA
THERE'S A REASON THEY CALL IT A SELF-MANAGED SUPER FUND

You **are the trustee of your super fund and** *you* **are ultimately responsible for your super fund. Not your accountant. Not your financial planner. Isn't that the best reason to take control? Just remember, with control comes responsibility.**

Things you need to remember about your beloved auditor

1. There should be no such thing as a $300 audit.

2. The two main risks I see in the audit of your super fund are the risk of cheap audits and the risk of independence.

3. Your auditor is the gatekeeper and safekeeper of your super fund.

4. There's a huge amount of training and experience that auditors have to gain to be able to audit your self-managed super fund.

5. If you are paying peanuts to have your audit done, guess who will probably be doing it? I haven't seen too many monkeys getting their university degrees.

6. Do you know whether your audit is being outsourced to somewhere outside of Australia? How comfortable do you feel about that?

7. What's the worst that can happen? Well, if the ATO perform an audit of your super fund and find issues, then you may be up for increased taxes and fines, which could wipe out half or more of your super fund balance.

8. The independence of your auditor is so important. It ensures that you achieve a completely objective audit and audit opinion on the compliance of your super fund. Remember the possible consequences of non-compliance.

9. Auditors are advisors in that they advise whether you actually *are* adhering to legislative requirements, so it is a very different but important role they play to your other trusted advisors.

10. Don't accept being part of the sausage factory of cheap audits.

CHAPTER 13

THE INEVITABLE AND THE UNEXPECTED – WHAT HAPPENS THEN?

IN CHAPTER 10, I covered the need for insurance and why it is important. Insurance is a form of contingency planning, or planning for the expected (death) and unexpected (becoming temporarily or permanently disabled, suffering from a trauma or becoming otherwise unable to work). I also covered what happens when there is a payout. In the case of death, I'd like to go further and discuss estate and succession planning, or what happens to the money or other assets of the member that are sitting in the super fund.

There are also other unexpected events that could occur that can't be insured for but which should still be considered and planned for. One of these is the potential for a breakdown in relationships between the members of the self-managed super fund, with the biggest issue being separation or divorce of members. It's the *why, how* and *what* that you need to know about here. *Why* planning for these events is important; *how* you plan for them; and *what* happens when the unexpected occurs. Here, I will only just scratch the surface of the complex area concerning estate and succession planning. There are solicitors who specialise in this area and you should give consideration to having them as an important part of your team. They could save you a whole lot of heartache, time and money.

THE INEVITABLE

Wouldn't you know, it's not totally straightforward. When a member of a super fund dies, among other things, there will be the need to deal with the balance in their super fund. This balance converts to what is known as a **death benefit,** which will, of course, constitute a **condition of release.** A death benefit has to be paid out as soon as is practical, which can have its complications where assets need to be sold.

An important thing to know here is that, when you die, your superannuation balance dose not automatically become part of your estate which is distributed according to your will.

It is the responsibility of the trustee/s to ensure that this is handled correctly. Guidance in relation to this is in the legislation as well as the all-important trust deed. I'm not suggesting that you go through this process alone as this could be a very emotional time, and it would be wise to seek the assistance of a solicitor, accountant and auditor to ensure that everything is handled properly from a legal and compliance perspective. However, like everything else in this book, I do think it is important that you understand an overview of the process, so you can have confidence that your advisors are doing the right thing.

A death benefit, which is paid to a **beneficiary** or beneficiaries, can only be paid out in three ways:

- As a lump sum to dependents;

- As an income stream to dependents; or

- As a lump sum to the estate (personal legal representative) of the member, where it will be distributed in accordance with the instructions in their will.

In relation to self-managed super funds a **dependent** is a spouse, child under 18 or anyone who has a disability or is financially dependent on the member who has died.

Where a lump sum is paid it is also possible for a super fund to pay an **anti-detriment payment** to a beneficiary. Now, I won't explain it in any great detail as there are many twists and turns in relation to this type of payment, and your financial advisor will be able to advise you on the mechanics of the actual payment, should the need arise. What I will explain however, is that it is a payment to compensate for the tax that has been paid by the deceased member on their contributions and related earnings while they were accumulating in the super fund. This rule was introduced when contributions tax was introduced as there was criticism that the tax was equivalent to a death tax. To compensate for this detriment, the lump sum paid to a beneficiary is effectively grossed up to equal the deceased member's balance had they not paid contributions tax. This is great for the beneficiary, however there are factors that need to be considered by the super fund such as how this additional payment will be funded. This is definitely one where you need to talk to your financial advisors but at least you've now heard of this term and know the basics.

As a member of your super fund, you should nominate who your beneficiary or beneficiaries will be for the payment of a death benefit. This nomination should be formally documented and signed and you should ensure that all the trustees of your super fund are given the document so they are aware of your wishes. There are different types of nominations, all with the all too familiar *eyes glaze over* names, which I will try and simplify for you.

The first is where you, as a member, are receiving an income stream/pension. In this case, you sign a **Reversionary Nomination,** which means that, on your death, the income stream is then paid to or reverts to your beneficiary, who is referred to as a **Reversionary Beneficiary.** If you don't nominate who your beneficiary is then the other trustees will decide who the beneficiaries are taking into account the requirements of the legislation. Alternatively the trustees may pay the benefits to your estate where it will be dealt with in accordance with your will.

Where you, as a member, are not receiving a pension or income stream and a Reversionary Nomination is, therefore, not in place, then the nomination of your beneficiary will be in the form of a **Binding Death Benefit Nomination** or a **Non-binding Death Benefit Nomination.**

A Binding Death Benefit Nomination will definitively set out who the beneficiary or beneficiaries are. There is a requirement that this needs to be renewed every three years (Lapsing Binding Death Benefit Nomination), unless your super fund trust deed permits it to be an indefinite nomination (Non - Lapsing Binding Death Benefit Nomination).

A **Non-binding Death Benefit Nomination** may nominate how some or all of the benefits from your super fund are distributed, however, the trustee/s will have discretion as to the distribution of your death benefit to your dependents, or to your estate if there are no dependents. They will, however, be aware of your wishes. If there are several related members/trustees in a fund, there might be issues with the trustees having this discretion. I would think having a bit more certainty would be the way to go.

Your super fund may have to deduct tax from any payment of a death benefit, depending on the age of the member who died, the beneficiary and whether any of the components of the deceased's super fund balance is taxable.

Your accountant or other advisors will be able to advise you in relation to the correct tax treatment.

THE UNEXPECTED

"That won't ever happen to me" mentality stops so many people from planning for when or if the "happily ever after" doesn't happen. You really do need to have a contingency plan in place in case the unexpected does happen. You may think that you don't need one and, if you don't, that's great. If you do end up needing one, however, and have a plan or resolution strategy in place, then this will cut out a lot of heartache for all concerned in what is a very emotional time. As with so many other strategies that have been covered in this book, the best place for this is in the trust deed.

The statistics show that one in three marriages ends in divorce. *De facto* relationships enjoy the same rules that govern marriage. The majority of self-managed super funds involve either married or *de facto* couples. They are often referred to as "Mum and Dad" funds. Unfortunately, separation and divorce do happen to couples with self-managed super funds.

Statistics also show that people are getting married later and staying married longer before becoming divorced. This means that there can be a larger pool of assets, including the money invested in super, that needs to be split. So the stakes are high.

When a couple separates or divorces, a property settlement process is initiated. This will involve all the marital assets, including the assets of a super fund. The property settlement process will decide the amount that each party will receive, which can be a dollar amount or a percentage split. Once that is decided, then further decisions can be made as to whether the assets of the super fund need to be split, transferred or sold. There are as many different scenarios as there are relationship break-ups, so I won't go into too much detail here.

If there is agreement that the assets need to be split, then this needs to be affected as soon as possible. The assets need to be either rolled over into an account in the relevant member's name in the super fund or transferred out to another super fund. It may not be possible to effect this transfer immediately because if, for example, the split involves business real property, that needs to be sold and the property is an integral part of the business of one or more of the members. A delay in the transfer is acceptable if there is an agreement in place whereby no benefits will be paid until the transfer is affected.

Some or all of the members may elect to stay or decide to leave the super fund. The decision to stay may be as a result of difficulty splitting assets. The example that I gave above of the business real property would fit into this category.

Having a divorced couple remain in a self-managed super fund could lead to issues, depending on how acrimonious the separation and/or divorce was. A classic and true example to illustrate this is the case of the Shail Superannuation Fund, which I wrote about in Chapter 2. For Mrs. Shail, remaining in the fund with her ex-husband had devastating consequences.

As always, there are the taxation implications inherent in this area. I guess by now I don't have to really tell you that you should seek advice from those trusted advisors.

DON'T FORGET...

The last thing I want to cover is what you need to do to make sure that your self-managed super fund continues to comply with the rules as set out in the legislation and, of course, the super fund's trust deed. Things to remember:

- If you leave the super fund, resign as a member and individual trustee or director of the corporate trustee.

- Prepare minutes for the super fund for all the decisions being made and the actions being taken.

- Change the trust deed to correctly reflect the trustee information.

- Notify the ATO of the change by submitting the relevant form.

- Where there is a corporate trustee, notify ASIC of the changes to the directors – yes, there will be a form to do this.

- If there will only be a single member remaining, ensure there is either a corporate trustee or another non-member trustee.

- If the super fund has individual members, change the ownership details in relation to any assets.

- If all members are leaving the super fund, wind up the super fund. You can refer to Chapter 6 for the process.

MANTRA
THERE'S A REASON THEY CALL IT A SELF-MANAGED SUPER FUND

You are the trustee of your super fund and *you* are ultimately responsible for your super fund. Not your accountant. Not your financial planner. Isn't that the best reason to take control? Just remember, with control comes responsibility.

Things you need to remember about estate and succession planning

THE INEVITABLE

1. When you die, your superannuation balance does not automatically become part of your estate which is distributed as part of your will.

2. When a member of a super fund dies, a **death benefit** paid to a **beneficiary** or beneficiaries can only be paid out in three ways:

   - As a lump sum to dependents;

   - As an income stream to dependents; or

   - As a lump sum to the estate (personal legal representative) of the member, where it will be distributed in accordance with the instructions in the will.

3. A lump sum can also include an anti-detriment payment which is compensation for the tax that has been paid by the deceased member.

4. As a member of your super fund you should nominate who your beneficiary or beneficiaries will be. The different types of nominations are:

- Reversionary Nomination – where an income stream is being paid that income stream then reverts to your nominated beneficiary;

- Binding Death Benefit Nomination;

- Non-binding Death Benefit Nomination.

THE UNEXPECTED

1. What happens if the unexpected happens? You really do need to have a contingency plan in place. As with so many other strategies that have been covered in this book, the best place for this is in the trust deed.

2. When a couple separates or divorces and a property settlement process is initiated, this will involve all the marital assets, including the assets of the super fund.

3. Once the property settlement is finalised, then further decisions can be made as to whether the assets of the super fund need to be split, transferred or sold.

4. If there is agreement that the assets need to be split, then this needs to be affected as soon as possible.

5. A delay in the transfer is acceptable if there is an agreement in place whereby no benefits will be paid until the transfer can be practically affected e.g. in the case of the sale of business real property.

6. Some or all of the members may elect to stay or decide to leave the super fund. Having a divorced couple remain in a self-managed super fund could lead to issues, depending on how acrimonious the separation and/or divorce was. Remember the Shails.

7. As always, there are the taxation implications, so seek advice.

8. Make sure that your self-managed super fund continues to comply with the rules as set out in the legislation and the super fund's trust deed.

CHAPTER 14

BUT... BUT... BUT...
NO BUTS ABOUT IT

So THIS PART of our journey comes to an end. At the start, we considered the "Buts:"

- But it's easier to leave it to the people who know;

- But it's so complicated with all that technical jargon, plus the government keeps changing the rules;

- But I don't think I have the time to manage it.

I hope through reading this book these "Buts" have been busted:

- Yes, in some ways it is easier to leave it to other people, however, you can't also outsource your responsibility. I hope you have realised the importance of being in control and making the decisions so it really feels like your advisors are working for you and not the other way around. Get to know them all – even your elusive auditor. Remember the mantra.

- Yes, it's complicated with all that technical jargon, and the government *does* keep changing the rules. But, hopefully, this book has gone a little of the way to demystifying the complicated world of self-managed super funds. You should now have an idea about the basics and what that jargon actually means, so you can ask the right questions and have confidence to take a more hands-on role in the management of your super fund. To build on that knowledge, you can access so much more information out there – all you have to do is "Google It." You'll be spoiled for choice.

  I want to make special mention of the resources that both the ATO and ASIC have in the area of self-managed super funds. The ATO have a series of booklets that cover the whole life-cycle of a self-managed super fund, from setting up to winding up and everything in between. These are available from their website. Alternatively, ask one your advisors to provide you with copies. They should be glad to. They are very easy to read and understand. ASIC has a website called Money Smart and this is also an invaluable source of easy-to-understand information about self-managed super funds.

- Yes, it will take time to manage, but the time-investment will diminish as you gain more confidence in managing your super fund. You are not doing it alone – you still have your trusted advisors. They should be a team, sharing your journey to retirement with you at the helm. And it will truly be time well spent, with the fantastic reward at the end of enjoying your retirement to the fullest.

You *can* have the confidence to proactively manage your self-managed super fund and I'd love to hear you say the words – **YES, I CAN!**

Here's to the best retirement you can hope for and dream of.

MANTRA
THERE'S A REASON THEY CALL IT A SELF-MANAGED SUPER FUND

You are the trustee of your super fund and *you* are ultimately responsible for your super fund. Not your accountant. Not your financial planner. Isn't that the best reason to take control? Just remember, with control comes responsibility.

THE AUTHOR

AUDREY DAWSON WAS born in Scotland and emigrated to Australia with her family in the 60's as one of the ten pound fares. She has been an accountant since 1985 and held many senior positions both in government and in the not for profit sector. Audrey has even been one of those lottery officials that you see on TV as part of the lotto draws. All her appearances probably added up to her 15 minutes of fame.

In 2011, Audrey commenced her own accounting practice, which has developed and morphed into Super Confidence, specialising in empowering owners of self-managed super funds, or those contemplating investing in one, to have the confidence to proactively manage their super fund. The Super Confidence motto is, in fact: "Yes You Can – Have the confidence to manage your own super fund."

Audrey is also a frustrated teacher who loves mentoring, teaching and empowering people. Writing a book is a great way to indulge that passion.

She lives in Brisbane, Queensland, with her husband Laurie and sons Sam and Jake.

To find out more about Audrey and Super Confidence please visit the website at www.superconfidence.com.au.

GLOSSARY – YOUR HANDY LITTLE GUIDE OF USEFUL INFORMATION

Term	What does it mean?	Where is it explained?
Account Based Pension	Between the ages of 55 to 60 and 64, if you decide that you don't want to work anymore, you can receive an income stream known as an account based pension. A minimum amount must be paid (currently 4% of account balance). No maximum amount needs to be paid. As a trustee of your super fund, you need to ensure that you have a written declaration stating that you as the member of your super fund have no intention of working again for more than 10 hours a week.	Chapter 5
Accumulation Phase and Account	While you are still working and contributing to your super fund as a member, this is known as the accumulation phase. Any contributions being made into the fund are classified in the super fund as being in the accumulation part of the super fund.	Chapter 4
Actuary and Actuarial Certificate	To work out the tax free or exempt current pension income, when a pension is to be paid, and members are in different phases and the funds are unsegregated, you, as trustee, will need to get an actuarial certificate from an actuary.	Chapter 5

Term	What does it mean?	Where is it explained?
Annuity	The super fund pays a lump sum or multiple amounts to an insurance company whilst your super fund is in accumulation phase. When you meet a condition of release, the insurance company will pay you an annual amount each year. This can be a fixed amount (same each year), indexed amount (increasing in line with inflation) or a variable amount (depending on what your lump sum has been invested in and the volatility and hence return of those investments). These are generally great if you want a bit of certainty.	Chapter 5
Anti-detriment Payment	A payment to compensate for the tax that has been paid by a deceased member on their contributions and related earnings while they were accumulating in the super fund. To compensate for this detriment, the lump sum paid to a beneficiary is effectively grossed up to equal the deceased member's balance had they not paid contributions tax.	Chapter 13
APRA Regulated Fund	Mainstream retail or industry super fund, which is regulated by the Australian Prudential Regulation Authority.	Chapter 1
Arm's Length	Dealings between two parties must be seen to be independent, above board and should not favour one party over the other.	Chapter 7
Auditor	Auditors are more than your necessary evil. To know us is to love us and, hopefully, by the end of the book, you'll be wondering where we've been all your life.	Chapter 12
Bare Trust or Security Trust	If a super fund borrows to buy property, it must be held in a separate trust called a bare trust or security trust. It's a 'bare' trust because it can barely do anything but hold the property in trust on behalf of your super fund until the loan is repaid.	Chapter 7
Beneficiary and Beneficial Ownership - LRBA	In relation to a limited recourse borrowing arrangement (LRBA), the bare trust holds property in trust for your super fund and your fund is therefore the beneficiary of the bare trust and beneficial owner of the property, subject to the LRBA.	Chapter 7

Term	What does it mean?	Where is it explained?
Beneficiary – Insurance	The person who will receive the payout from the fund's insurance. As the policies are in the name of your super fund, the fund will receive the payout. Once a condition of release is established, the monies then need to be paid out to the member, or to the person nominated by the member (where it is a life insurance payout).	Chapter 10
Beneficiary – Death Benefit	Where nomination by the member, the beneficiary will be either a dependent or a personal legal representative (if the member wishes the benefit to be paid to their estate and be dealt with in accordance with the instructions of their will). Where no nomination by the member, it will be at the discretion of the trustee as to the distribution to any dependents.	Chapter 13
Binding Nomination – Life Insurance Payout	In the case of a life insurance payout, the member nominates who will be the beneficiary of the proceeds.	Chapter 10
Binding Death Benefit Nomination	Written nomination by the member of the super fund, which definitively sets out who the beneficiary/s are. There is a requirement that this needs to be renewed every three years unless your super fund trust deed permits it to be an indefinite nomination. The nomination needs to be provided to the trustees so that they are aware of the member's wishes.	Chapter 13
Capital Gains and Capital Gains Tax	When your super fund has an investment and decides to sell it while you are in the accumulation phase, then, if it has increased in value, your fund will have made a capital gain and you will have to pay tax on the profit that your super fund makes. Capital gains tax is not applicable for those assets that are being used to fund any retirement benefits that are being paid by your super fund.	Chapter 4

Term	What does it mean?	Where is it explained?
Capital Loss	If your super fund sells an investment and the amount received is less than what is recorded in the financial records of your super fund, it makes a capital loss. Your super fund cannot claim the loss and can only offset the loss against a capital gain. Where this occurs, you will have to carry forward the loss until you can offset it against a capital gain. Your accountant will know how to account for this and what to include in the super fund tax return.	Chapter 4
Collectibles or Personal Use Assets	The following come under the umbrella of collectibles or personal use assets: Artwork Jewellery Antiques Artefacts Coins, medallions or bank notes Postage stamps or first day covers Rare folios, manuscripts or books Memorabilia Wine or spirits Motor vehicles Recreational boats Memberships of sporting or social clubs The big rule is that you or a related party can't enjoy these collectibles whilst you are in your accumulation phase. So you or a related party can't wear the jewellery, hang the art in your home or office, drink the wine, drive the car or sail the boat.	Chapter 4
Complying Fund	Your super fund is following and adhering to the rules, which are detailed in the Superannuation Industry (Supervision) Act 1993 and Superannuation Industry (Supervision) Regulations 1994 (see Appendix B).	Chapter 2

Term	What does it mean?	Where is it explained?
Condition of Release	When you reach your preservation age or over, you can access your super. By doing so you will have met a condition of release. A condition of release can also be death, terminal illness, permanent incapacity (any occupation) or temporary incapacity (where an insurance policy has been purchased and an insurance payout has been received).	Chapter 5 Chapter 10
Contributions – Different Types Concessional Non-concessional	**Concessional contributions** Mandatory contributions or super guarantee contributions paid in by your employer. Salary sacrificing, where you as an employee can have part of your salary paid into superannuation. Self-employed contributions Personal contributions where a tax deduction is or will be claimed. For these types of contributions, a tax deduction has usually been claimed and these are taxed in the self-managed super fund. **Non-concessional contributions** Personal contributions where a tax deduction will not been claimed . Government co-contributions – presently, if you are classified as a low income earner and make personal contributions into superannuation, then the government will match up to $500, of the contribution you have made. Spouse contributions – as the name suggests, these are contributions made by a spouse of the member. In-specie contributions – contributions made in a form other than cash. The super fund doesn't have to pay tax on these contributions.	Chapter 3
Contribution Caps	Limits as to the amount of concessional and non-concessional contributions that can be paid into your super fund.	Chapter 3

Term	What does it mean?	Where is it explained?
Contributions Reserve	It is possible for contributions to be initially posted to an unallocated contribution account or contributions reserve account before being allocated to a member's account within 28 days. Why is this important? Given this time frame, it is possible to make concessional contributions in excess of the contribution cap at the end of a financial year and not be penalised.	Chapter 3
Contribution Splitting	It is possible for a member of a fund, where his/her spouse is also a member of the same fund and not retired, to split their contributions.	Chapter 3
Contribution Splitting Contribution	Contributions as a result of a member assigning their concessional contributions (less contributions tax) to their spouse. It only happens once a year and always in the financial year following that in which the contributions were paid in.	Chapter 3
Corporate Trustee	Where a company is the trustee of the super fund and all members of the self-managed super fund are directors of the company.	Chapter 2
Death Benefit	When a member of a super fund dies, among other things, there will be the need to deal with the super fund balance that is sitting in their super fund. This is known as a death benefit and will, of course, constitute a condition of release.	Chapter 13
Dependent	For the purposes of the payout of a death benefit, this will be a spouse, children under 18 or anyone who was financially dependent on the member who has died.	Chapter 13
Exempt Current Pension Income	When your super fund goes into pension phase, any income earned on the balance that is in the pension account is not taxable and is classified as exempt current pension income.	Chapter 5
Franking Credits/ Imputation Credits	If your super fund invests in Australian listed company shares, the company may pay tax on its earnings and this will be reflected in the dividend statement as a franking credit. This is included in the earnings of your super fund and 15% tax is paid. Your super fund can then claim the entire franking credit as a deduction.	Chapter 4

194

Term	What does it mean?	Where is it explained?
Government Co-contribution	If you are classified as a low income earner and you make personal contributions into superannuation, then the government will match up to $500 of the contribution you have made.	Chapter 3
In-house Assets	An in-house asset is any of the following: A loan to, or an investment in a related party of your fund; An investment in a related trust of your fund; An asset of your fund that is leased to a related party. In general, as a trustee, you are restricted from lending to, investing in or leasing to a related party of your fund more than 5% of your fund's total assets. *(Australian Taxation Office Publication – "Running a Self-Managed Super Fund.").*	Chapter 3
In-specie Contributions	Contributions not in the form of money. Examples are: Shares that are listed on an approved exchange such as the Australian Stock Exchange; Commercial property, which is also known as business real property; Units in widely held unit trusts; Assets from a member or related party of the trust (in-house assets), where the value is not greater than 5% of the super fund's asset value.	Chapter 3

Term	What does it mean?	Where is it explained?
Insurance	If you are in an APRA regulated superannuation fund (retail or industry main stream fund) you have a certain level of insurance coverage. Switch to a self-managed super fund and you don't. It's not compulsory for your super fund to have insurance for the members – what is compulsory is that you, as trustee, should consider it. This has to be part of your documented investment strategy. Why are you insuring? To cover circumstances that will severely affect your ability to continue to contribute to your super fund and, therefore, the ability of your super fund to service debt and pay other expenses.	Chapter 10
Investment Strategy	Your vital and well-thought-out plan, made so that you can enjoy your retirement to the fullest. Reviewed annually, it needs to consider risk, returns, diversification, liquidity and insurance for members.	Chapter 9
Loan-to-value Ratio	If your super fund is considering borrowing, the lender will want your fund to contribute a percentage of the value of the property and will lend the super fund the remaining percentage. If the lender is willing to lend, for example, 65%, then this is the loan-to-value ratio.	Chapter 7
Limited Recourse Borrowing Arrangement (LRBA)	If your super fund borrows to buy property and defaults on the loan, then the action (recourse) that the lender can take is limited to repossessing the asset that the borrowing relates to and they can't touch anything else in your super fund.	Chapter 7
Mandatory contributions	Also known as super guarantee contributions, these are the compulsory contributions that your employer must pay	Chapter 3
Market Value	The amount for which something can be sold in a given market, thus giving an unbiased or independent value of the asset.	Chapter 3

Term	What does it mean?	Where is it explained?
Member	Members contribute to the fund and reap the benefits upon retirement. There are rules as to how many members can be in a super fund (at present the maximum number of members is four).	Chapter 2
	All members must be either an individual trustee or a director of the corporate trustee. All trustees do not, however, have to be members. e.g. for a single member fund, there must be two trustees and one of these can be a non-member.	
Member's Statement	Annual statement prepared for each member of your super fund. The information contained in the member's statement includes:	Chapter 2
	Opening balance;	
	Increase in member's account during the financial year from such things as contributions, transfers in and share of net earnings;	
	Decrease in member's account during the year from such things as tax, benefits paid and insurance policy premiums paid;	
	Closing balance;	
	Classification of closing balance into preserved, restricted non-preserved and unrestricted non-preserved; and	
	Tax free and taxable components.	
Net Income or Earnings	Money earned through your super fund's investments, less expenses you can claim in the course of earning that money. Where the super fund is in accumulation phase, the super fund will have to pay 15% tax on these net income or earnings.	Chapter 4
Non-binding Death Benefit Nomination	A member may nominate how some or all of the benefits from the super fund are distributed, however, the trustee/s will have discretion as to the distribution of your death benefit. They will be aware of your wishes.	Chapter 13

Term	What does it mean?	Where is it explained?
Non-complying Fund	Where your super fund is not adhering to the rules, which are detailed in the Superannuation Industry (Supervision) Act 1993 and Superannuation Industry (Supervision) Regulations 1994 (see Appendix B). When the ATO finds out, you can be classified as a non-complying fund and that means the super fund can be taxed at a very high rate (at present 45%).	Chapter 3
Non-preserved Funds	There are no or very few restrictions on your super fund paying these funds to you. They are classified as restricted non-preserved or unrestricted non-preserved.	Chapter 4
PAYG Payment Summary	This annual summary lists the pension or income stream payments made and the tax withheld and is equivalent to the group certificate that you receive from your employer. As a member receiving the benefit, this is included your personal tax return.	Chapter 5
PAYG Withholding Tax.	If tax is being withheld from pension or income stream payments made to relevant members, then your super fund needs to register for pay as you go withholding tax with the ATO. Any tax being withheld is then paid to the ATO. At the end of the financial year, your super fund will need to issue a payment summary to the relevant member.	Chapter 5
Pension Phase and Account	When you are eligible to access your super fund and you nominate to do so, your super fund is classed as being in the pension phase. The balance of the portion of your super fund that will be used to pay the pension is classed as your pension account.	Chapter 5
Personal Contributions	Additional amounts you personally pay into superannuation.	Chapter 3
Preservation Age	This is the age at which you can access your super. At present, this is between 55 and 60, depending on the year you where born.	Chapter 5

Term	What does it mean?	Where is it explained?
Preservation Rule	From 1 July 1999, while you are in the accumulation phase, your funds are classified as preserved, which means you can't have access to them.	Chapter 4
Preserved Funds	Prior to you being able to access your super, your super fund is in the accumulation phase and your funds are classed as preserved, which means you can't touch them or have access to them.	Chapter 4
Proportioning Rule	Whatever the tax free and taxable percentages are that make up the balance that is to be paid as a benefit, these will be the percentages that will be utilised to work out the taxable portion of the benefit payment.	Chapter 5
Related Parties	Spouse, relatives, any partnerships that you might be in, as well as trusts and companies that you or other members of the fund controls.	Chapter 4
Restricted Non-preserved Funds	Any contributions paid into super prior to 1 July 1999. You can access these if you meet a condition of release or when you cease working for an employer who was making those contributions for you prior to 1 July 1999. So if you were working for an employer prior to 1 July 1999 and resigned after that date then you can access any benefits paid prior to 1 July 1999.	Chapter 4
Reversionary Beneficiary	Where you as a member are receiving an income stream/pension, on your death, the income stream is then paid to or reverts to your beneficiary, who is referred to as a reversionary beneficiary.	Chapter 13
Reversionary Nomination	If you are receiving an income stream/ pension from your super fund, you should sign a form nominating who is to be the beneficiary (reversionary beneficiary). On your death, the income stream is then paid to or reverts to your reversionary beneficiary.	Chapter 13

Term	What does it mean?	Where is it explained?
Rollover or Transfer In	Transfer of the balance of your superannuation from another superannuation fund into your self-managed super fund. There are no barriers like age or employment status to being able to rollover into a self-managed super fund and the same rules apply as to being able to access these funds, i.e. you will not be able to access this balance until you are entitled to, which is called a condition of release. Don't forget the inevitable form that you will have to fill out and this is available from the Australian Tax Office website. This form is presently called *"Rollover initiation requires to transfer whole balance of superannuation benefit to your self-managed super fund."*	Chapter 3
Salary Sacrificing	Where you, as an employee, can also choose to have part of your salary paid into superannuation.	Chapter 3
Segregated	Where part of your super fund is in pension phase, and the assets that make up the pension account can be separately identified	Chapter 5
Self-employed Contributions	If you are self-employed, you are not required to contribute to a super fund, however, you may choose to do so.	Chapter 3
Single Acquirable Asset	Your super fund can only borrow to purchase one asset. It could be land, a land and house package or a parcel of shares in one company.	Chapter 7
Sole Purpose Test	Ensuring that the fund is being maintained for the sole purpose of providing for the member/s' retirement.	Chapter 2
Spouse Contributions	Contributions made by your spouse, which can attract a tax rebate for the person making the contribution.	Chapter 3

Term	What does it mean?	Where is it explained?
Superannuation Industry (Supervision) Act 1993 and Superannuation Industry (Supervision) Regulations 1994.	Relevant overarching legislative rules that dictate how self-managed super funds are to operate. See Appendix B for the really important parts.	Chapter 2
Super Guarantee Contributions	Generally, if you work for someone, they have to pay a certain percentage of your salary in the form of superannuation. There may be exceptions and, presently, these are where you earn under $450 a month, are a part-time employee under 18, or are over 70.	Chapter 3
Taxable Component of your Super Fund Balance	This relates to the concessional contributions such as employer contributions, salary sacrificing, personal contributions where you are claiming or plan to claim a tax deduction and self-employed contributions, as well as any share of net earnings and tax and expenses directly attributable to you as a member. A deduction has been claimed on these contributions and the only tax that has been paid is by the super fund, which is a low rate of tax.	Chapter 4

Term	What does it mean?	Where is it explained?
Taxation	There's nothing surer. Concessional contributions – whatever concessional contributions are paid into a super fund, there is 15% tax payable on these. Non-concessional contributions – a tax deduction has not been claimed on these contributions and this means that the super fund doesn't have to pay tax on these contributions. Your super fund is hopefully earning money through its investments. You can claim the expenses that you incur in the course of making these earnings. This gives the net earnings of your fund. Again, the super fund will have to pay 15% tax on these net earnings. If your super fund is in pension phase there is no tax payable on the earnings of the assets that form the funds used to pay the pension.	Chapter 4
Tax File Number (TFN)	As trustee, you need to make sure that you, as a member of the fund (remember those different roles and responsibilities), provide your TFN to the super fund. If you don't, then you, as trustee are not able to accept contributions – these have to be immediately returned if you don't receive the TFN within 30 days.	Chapter 3
Tax Free Component of Super Fund Balance	The tax free component comprises the member's non-concessional contributions, which incorporates personal contributions where a tax deduction has not been claimed, government co-contributions, spouse contributions and in-specie contributions. Given that the relevant amount of tax has been paid on these prior to them being contributed to your super fund, there will be no further tax payable on these.	Chapter 4

202

Term	What does it mean?	Where is it explained?
Transition to Retirement Income Stream	If you are between your preservation age and 64 and still working and you want to access your super, your super fund will pay you a transition to retirement income stream based on a percentage of the balance of your super fund. There are minimum and maximum percentages that can be paid (at present, the minimum is 4% and the maximum is 10%).	Chapter 5
Trust Account	A self-managed super fund is a trust account because the money in there is to be kept or held in trust for you until you retire. So it's your money, but it's not *really* your money until you retire.	Chapter 1 Chapter 2
Trust Deed	Each and every super fund needs to have its own set of rules and this comes in the form of a trust deed.	Chapter 2
Trustee	The self-managed super fund trust account is looked after by people who are called trustees. You can be a trustee as an individual, or your accountant may have set up a company and the company is the trustee of the super fund (known as a corporate trustee). Where a company is set up as a trustee, you will be a director of the company, along with any other members of the super fund. As trustee, your role is to ensure that the super fund is adhering to the legislative rules and regulations and to ensure that the fund is being maintained and managed for the sole purpose of providing for the member/s' retirement.	Chapter 1 Chapter 2
Trustee Declaration Form	To be a trustee of your super fund, you have to sign a trustee declaration form. The declaration aims to ensure that new trustees (or directors of corporate trustees) understand their obligations and responsibilities.	Chapter 2

Term	What does it mean?	Where is it explained?
Trustee Representation Letter	Letter provided to your super fund auditor as part of the annual audit. This letter makes representations in relation to: Sole purpose test Trustees' status (not disqualified) Trust deed, trustees' responsibilities and fund conduct Investment strategy Accounting policies Fund books and records Fraud, error and non-compliance Asset compliance and valuation Uncorrected misstatements Ownership and pledging of assets Related parties Borrowings Subsequent events Outstanding legal action Going concern Any other additional matters that you, as trustee, consider that your auditor should be aware of.	Chapter 12
Unrestricted Non-preserved	There are no restrictions on the super fund paying these funds to you. This happens when you reach 65 or have previously met a condition of release but have chosen not to take the funds.	Chapter 4
Unsegregated	In your super fund, there may be a member who is in pension phase and a member who is in accumulation phase. These accounts need to be segregated to work out the tax free and taxable components. They are usually not kept separate and the balance of your super fund is termed as being unsegregated.	Chapter 5

Term	What does it mean?	Where is it explained?
Untaxed Element	Contributions where there has been no tax paid e.g. Proceeds of an insurance claim where a tax deduction has been claimed on premiums paid Rolling over of defined benefits Taxed at 15% when they are received into the super fund	Chapter 4

COMPLIANCE REQUIREMENTS – WHAT YOUR AUDITOR REVIEWS

This appendix lists the 29 Sections and Regulations of the **Superannuation Industry (Supervision) Act 1993 and Superannuation Industry (Supervision) Regulations 1994,** which trustees of self-mananged super funds need to ensure they adhere to. Also included are the points that your auditor will or should consider when they are performing the audit of your self-managed super fund:

Section or Regulation	What is the section about?	What will your auditor look at?
S17A	The fund must meet the definition of an SMSF	Your auditor will check: Fund has fewer than 5 members; Each member is a trustee or a director of corporate trustee; If a 1 member fund, there is either a corporate trustee or another trustee; Trustees are not paid for any services provided to your super fund; Members aren't in an employer/employee relationship, unless they are related; None of the trustees have been disqualified, i.e. been convicted of an offence or insolvent or bankrupt. Your auditor will usually get you to confirm this in a trustee representation letter
S35A	The trustees must keep and maintain proper accounting records for a minimum of five years	Your auditor will agree the figures in your accounting records (ledger and trial balance) and supporting documents like invoices and bank statements to the financial statements and tax return. All the records that are provided to your auditor need to be able to be audited easily and properly. Believe me, your auditor really appreciates this. Your auditor will usually get you to confirm in the trustee representation letter that your super fund has kept these records for five years.
S35B	The trustees must prepare financial statements and maintain these for five years	Your auditor will check that the super fund has a statement of financial position (balance sheet) and an operating statement (profit & loss statement) and will again get you to confirm that these have been kept for five years.

Section or Regulation	What is the section about?	What will your auditor look at?
S35C(2)	The trustees must provide the auditor with the necessary documents to complete the audit in a timely and professional manner; and within 14 days of a written request from the auditor	This is a self-explanatory requirement, but probably one, as trustee, you were not aware of.
S52(2)(d)	The assets of the SMSF must be held separately from any assets held by the trustee personally or by a standard employer sponsor or an associate of the standard employer sponsor	Your auditor will check that all documents belonging to your super fund, e.g. bank statements, invoices, property title documents, are in the name of the super fund and not your own name. This will either be: The XYZ Super Fund; Mr X and Mrs X as trustees for the XYZ Super Fund (individual trustees); ABC Pty Ltd as trustee for the XYZ Super Fund (corporate trustee).
S52 (2)(e)	The trustee must not enter into a contract that would prevent/hinder them from exercising the powers of a trustee	As trustee, you need to always be able to freely exercise your duties so that the interests of the members of the super fund are protected and not compromised. Again, you, as trustee will confirm this in the trustee representation letter to your auditor.
S62	The fund must be maintained for the sole purpose of providing benefits to any or all of the following: fund members upon their retirement fund members upon reaching a prescribed age the dependants of a fund member in the case of the member's death before retirement	Your auditor will check: The trust deed of your super fund states that this is the purpose of the fund; Your super fund is not providing any financial assistance to its members or their relatives or allows any of the members to have private use of the assets of the super fund prior the member being entitled, i.e. having satisfied a condition of release; Payments from the super fund are only made after a member has satisfied a condition of release.

Section or Regulation	What is the section about?	What will your auditor look at?
S65	The trustees must not loan monies or provide financial assistance to any member or relative at any time during the financial year	Again, probably self-explanatory. Your auditor will check during the audit that there have been no payments of this nature. Payment of pensions or income streams, when you as a member have satisfied a condition of release, is okay as this is an allowable payment out of your super fund and what your super fund is all about.
S66	The trustees must not acquire any assets, that are not allowed, from any member or related party of the fund	Your auditor will check the supporting documentation in relation to the purchase of any assets to make sure the super fund is not purchasing from the member or a related party. Remember, from Chapter 3 - BPK#9 In specie contributions – the following are exceptions: Shares that are listed on an approved exchange such as the Australian Stock Exchange; Commercial property, which is also known as business real property; Units in widely held unit trusts; Assets from a member or related party of the trust (in-house assets), where the value is not greater than 5% of the super funds asset value.

Section or Regulation	What is the section about?	What will your auditor look at?
S67	The trustees of the fund must not borrow any money or maintain an existing borrowing (not listed as an exemption)	Your auditor will check any unusual transactions in your bank account that may indicate this is the case. As a word of warning, if your super fund bank account is inadvertently overdrawn, e.g. by a direct debit that should not have been paid out, and you, as trustee, realise it and quickly rectify it, this still is technically a breach of S67. The exemptions relate to paying out a beneficiary, settling a securities transaction, paying a surcharge obligation or borrowing under S67A (limited recourse borrowing arrangement).
S67A-67B	These sections cover the rules in relation to a limited-recourse borrowing arrangement (LRBA)	Your auditor will check that everything that I covered in Chapter 7 is in place with regard to an LRBA.
S69-71E	Rules relating to in-house assets I covered in-house assets in Chapter 3 and these are any of the following: a loan to, or an investment in a related party of your fund; an investment in a related trust of your fund; an asset of your fund that is leased to a related party. In general, as a trustee, you are restricted from lending to, investing in or leasing to a related party of your fund more than 5% of your fund's total assets. *(Australian Taxation Office Publication – "Running a Self-Managed Super Fund").*	If there appear to be any transactions of this nature, your auditor will review the supporting documentation that relate to these transactions and will seek more information to determine if there has been a breach.

Section or Regulation	What is the section about?	What will your auditor look at?
S73-75	In-house assets must be valued by trustees and these sections outline the rules in relation to these valuations, which in the main insist that the valuation must be at arms-length	Your auditor will be looking for a written valuation that satisfies the rules that it is an independent or arms-length valuation.
S80-85	The trustees must comply with the in-house asset rules, which are outlined in S69-71E	If there appear to be any transactions of this nature, your auditor will review the supporting documentation that relate to these transactions and will seek more information to determine if there has been a breach.
S103	The trustees must keep minutes of all meetings and retain the minutes for a minimum of 10 years	As trustee, you will confirm that you have done this in the trustee representation letter that your auditor will require you to sign.
S104A	Trustees who became a trustee on or after 1 July 2007 must sign and retain a trustee declaration	Your auditor will require a copy of this document.
S109	All investment transactions must be made and maintained at arms-length – that is, purchase, sale price and income from an asset reflects a true market value/rate of return	Your auditor will be looking at the documentation that supports these transactions and will ask further questions or seek further advice or documentation from you as trustee.
S126K	A disqualified person cannot be a trustee, investment manager or custodian of a superannuation fund. The ATO or the Federal Court of Australia will disqualify a person from acting as trustee of a super fund	As trustee, you will confirm that you are not a disqualified person in the trustee representation letter that your auditor will require you to sign.

Section or Regulation	What is the section about?	What will your auditor look at?
Sub Reg 1.06 (9A)	Pension payments must be made at least annually, and the minimum must be paid	Where your super fund has paid out a pension, your auditor will check that the amount paid out satisfies the minimum requirements. This is based on the minimum percentage and also that more than one payment has been made (must be a series of payments).
Reg 4.09	Trustees must formulate, regularly review and give effect to an investment strategy for the fund	Your auditor will want to check that you have an investment strategy and that it covers all the things I spoke about in Chapter 9. Not only does your super fund have to have an investment strategy, it also has to stick (give effect) to it.
Reg 5.03	Investment returns must be allocated to members in a manner that is fair and reasonable	Allocation of contributions and investment returns were covered in Chapter 4 (BPK#16). The preparation of annual individual member's statements is required to reflect these. Your auditor will check the calculations behind the figures included in each of the member's statements to ensure that they are fair and reasonable.
Reg 5.08	Member benefits must be maintained in the fund until transferred, rolled over, allotted (to the member's spouse) or cashed in a permitted fashion	Your auditor will check that any payments out of the fund are allowable.
Reg 6.17	Payments of member benefits must be made in accordance with Part 6 or Part 7A of the regulations and be permitted by the trust deed	Payments of member benefits were covered in Chapter 5 and are based on the rules that are detailed in Part 6 and Part 7A of the Superannuation Industry (Supervision) Regulations 1994. Your auditor will check that any payments of benefits satisfy these rules and are allowable under the super fund's trust deed.

Section or Regulation	What is the section about?	What will your auditor look at?
Reg 7.04	Contributions can only be accepted in accordance with the applicable rules for the year being audited	Your auditor will check: The trust deed allows the type of contributions that are being made; If you pass the work test where you are above 65 but below 75; Only compulsory employer contributions are being accepted; Concessional and non-concessional contributions do not exceed the allowed limits; If excessive non-concessional contributions are received then these are returned to the contributor within 30 days of the super fund becoming aware of the excess; Contributions are returned within 30 days where a member has not notified the super fund of their tax file number.
Reg 8.02B	When preparing accounts and statements required by subsection 35B(1) of the Act, an asset must be valued at its market value	Your super fund needs to revalue its assets by the end of the financial year and this needs to be reflected in the financial statements of your super fund. Your auditor will check that this has been performed. Shares will be valued at the share price as at 30 June each year. For property, a valuation by a real estate agent or a review of similar properties in the area will suffice. The value of cash will not alter.
Reg 13.12	Trustees must not recognise an assignment of a super interest of a member or beneficiary	You, as trustee, cannot recognise, or in any way encourage or sanction an assignment of, or charge over, a beneficiary's interest in your super fund. This will be confirmed by you in the trustee representation letter you provide to your auditor.

Section or Regulation	What is the section about?	What will your auditor look at?
Reg 13.13	Trustees must not recognise a charge over or in relation to a member's benefits	Same as Reg 13.12, with the same confirmation process.
Reg 13.14	Trustees must not give a charge over, or in relation to, an asset of the fund	An example of this is where a mortgage is put on a property that is owned outright by your super fund and this is not allowed. Your auditor will seek confirmation in the trustee representation letter that you provide to them. They will also undertake a property search to ensure that there are no mortgages on the property (a mortgage in relation to a limited recourse borrowing arrangement is okay).
Reg 13.18AA	Investments in collectables and personal use assets must be maintained in accordance with prescribed rules	I covered Collectible and Personal Use Assets in Chapter 4 (BPK#14) and your auditor will check that your super fund is following those rules. The main ones are: You or a related party can't wear the jewellery, hang the art in your home or office, drink the wine, drive the car or sail the boat. That can't happen until you retire. There are now new rules that your super fund has to have them insured within a week of purchase. Your super fund has to have them valued annually and has to organise suitable storage for them and this can't be at your home or office. Your auditor will look for written proof of where you store the collectible, as well as documentation of the reasons for the decision on where you decided to store it.

www.ingramcontent.com/pod-product-compliance
Lightning Source LLC
Chambersburg PA
CBHW070910270326
41927CB00011B/2521